DOMINIQUE'S KITCHEN

Easy everyday Asian-inspired food

Dominique Woolf

Photography by *Richard Clatworthy*

MICHAEL  JOSEPH

For my husband **Gordon**
and our three expert food tasters,
Logan, **Florence** and **Grace**.

Contents

Foreword by Jamie Oliver

—

Writing a book is no mean feat, and when we started *The Great Cookbook Challenge* TV show, as well as the excitement and glamour of the publishing deal that awaited the winner, we knew that there was an incredible amount of hard work and slog ahead of them, too. Dominique has done an astounding job – not only is it the first cookbook she's ever written, she's done it in record time.

In this book, you'll get honest, humble, utterly delicious food, inspired by brilliant ingredients and flavours from across Asia. The recipes are super achievable and I know first hand that Dominique has really put in the hours to perfect each recipe and make sure that it will deliver for you, at home. That's what's brilliant about Dominique's approach – she's busy, just like the rest of us, running her own successful business and parenting three adorable kids, and she needs to get good food on the table, fast.

Her enthusiasm and quiet work ethic shone through from day one, and she's a worthy winner. So, read on, enjoy and get cooking!

It's not often that time stands still. But that's what happened when I stood there, in the final of *The Great Cookbook Challenge with Jamie Oliver*, at the end of a whirlwind experience, my mum and husband beside me, hoping that my name would be called out.

Ever since my Dutch grandmother, Granny Woolf, bought me my first ever cookbook when I was 9, I've harboured a secret desire to write my own. I could never have predicted it would manifest in quite the way it did – I mean, we've all watched TV competitions, and the idea I would actually win one is quite mind-boggling.

Presenting the judges with my humble traybake on the very first challenge in round one, I wondered whether I was out of my league. Regretting the decision not to do something more elaborate, I held my breath as they tasted it. I never could have guessed that my Tamarind, honey & sesame chicken (page 65), in all its beige glory, would help propel me on the trip of a lifetime.

To have a panel of respected food experts taste your cooking is a daunting prospect for anyone – let alone me, a messy, somewhat chaotic home cook. Week after week, my nerves were frayed as I gave it my all. Somehow, miraculously, I got through to the final. Having Jamie as our mentor was pretty surreal as well. *The Naked Chef* was the first food TV programme I ever watched over 20 years ago, and Jamie's books and recipes have played a huge part in my cooking and my development as a writer. I still can't believe it.

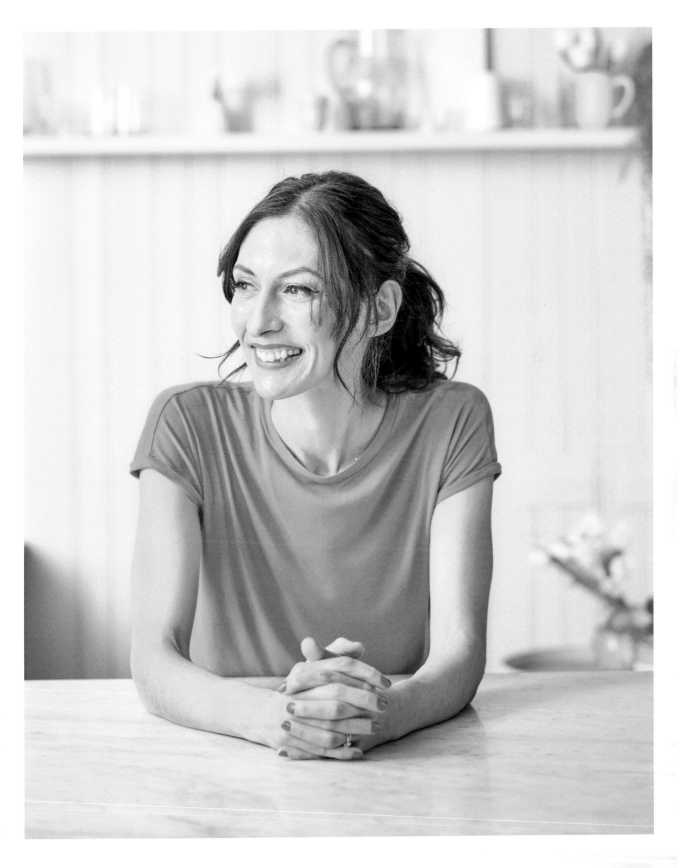

Food has always been my biggest passion, my sunshine on a cloudy day. Pre-kids I greedily ate my way around London, exploring every cuisine I possibly could at any opportunity. Holidays were only ever about eating (OK, and maybe getting a bit of sunshine!) – that heady feeling of standing in a street food market in Bangkok or in a pintxo bar in San Sebastián. Just intoxicating.

Now, with a young family, both eating out and travelling are rarities. Cooking has become an integral part of my life – my way of exploring the world without leaving the kitchen.

From an early age, my Thai mother fed my brother and me satay, stir-fries and noodles. I vividly remember the smell of red curry filling the house, even though it was too hot for us to eat. She taught me the importance of tasting food throughout the cooking process, and always making sure there was balance – 'a little sweet, a little salty, a little spicy'.

Thai and Asian-inspired cuisine is unsurprisingly where I naturally lean. It is my midweek go-to, my perfect comfort food, my special night out. To me, whipping up a cheat's curry or a last-minute stir-fry is second nature, but in chatting to friends I realized this wasn't the case for everyone. They would tell me how much they loved food from across Asia, from fragrant curries to flavourful stir-fries, but that cooking these dishes felt daunting; they had no idea where to start. That planted a seed that grew into the concept for this book.

I wanted to show people just how easy it is to use some of these much-loved flavours in their everyday cooking. This is not about recreating traditional dishes – I wanted to share the kind of meals I cook at home, inspired by my Thai mum and auntie and my granny (who was raised in Indonesia), as well as my travels over the years. I want to spread the joy of eating delicious home-cooked food.

Like many of you, I know what it's like to be busy, home late or over-tired, when cooking from scratch is the last thing on your mind. I know what it's like to be stuck in a food rut – we've all been there!

What I want more than anything is to inspire you to get cooking and for you to feel that same spark of excitement when eating as I do. I hope you'll find my recipes easy to follow, and achievable on any night of the week. They're all simple to make, packed with exciting flavours, and I hope they'll help you fall more in love with Asian-inspired cuisine.

This book started life in the most unusual of ways and I can't tell you how privileged I feel to be writing it. What a journey it's been so far – I sincerely hope it's just the beginning.

Pantry Essentials

In order to create the recipes in this book, you'll need to hunt out a few slightly more specialist ingredients. Most you'll find in the supermarket, and all are easily available in Asian shops or online. Once you have these ingredients in your possession, the world really will be your oyster sauce.

An important consideration to me in writing this book is to maximize the use you'll get out of those ingredients. There's nothing more annoying than having half a jar of paste languishing at the back of your fridge for five months with no purpose. I have tried to give you at least a couple of recipes for each specialist ingredient where I can, to help you make the most of each purchase. So if you are flicking through the book and wondering why there are four miso recipes, for example, now you know! It's to give you the best value and to make your storecupboard work for you.

Chilli bean paste

Known as doubanjiang or toban djan, this salty Sichuan chilli bean paste is made from fermented soybeans, broad beans and chillies. Used in cooking, it gives a savoury, umami-filled depth to dishes. Available online or in Asian supermarkets.

Chilli oil with bits

It's the bits that we're interested in, so get a good one! We're after flavour and texture, not just oil. I always use my own version called Chilli Crunch, available from The Woolf's Kitchen.

Chillies

Bird's-eye chilli – a small chilli used in Thai cuisine. Much hotter than the standard red chilli, so feel free to swap if you prefer less heat.

Red chillies – when listed in a recipe, these refer to the standard red chillies you buy in the supermarket or greengrocer's. The heat level is mild to medium.

All fresh chillies can be frozen and used straight from the freezer.

Dried red chilli flakes – these add a roasted flavour to dishes. Unlike chilli powder, these flakes are not mixed with other ingredients.

Whole dried chillies – these are available in some supermarkets, online or in Asian shops. They add a wonderful roasted flavour to dishes.

Chinese 5-spice

A blend of 5 spices – star anise, cinnamon, fennel seeds, black pepper and cloves. Used frequently in Chinese cooking, it adds a deeply aromatic layer of flavour. Also available as a 'seasoning' mix with added ingredients such as salt, onion and garlic powder.

Coconut milk

A core ingredient in many Southeast Asian dishes and recipes in this book. Most commonly available brands have stabilizers in them, which makes them slightly more gloopy. They're fine to use but if you are able to get hold of one which has no extra additives, such as Biona, then all the better. I personally always use full-fat coconut milk as I find the taste and texture far better than the light version. Leftovers can be frozen.

Fish sauce

A key seasoning ingredient in Southeast Asian cuisine and widely available. If you aren't familiar with it, don't be put off by its pungent smell – it delivers a big hit of umami-saltiness that's vital in many dishes.

Gochujang paste

A Korean fermented red chilli paste that adds a spicy, sweet savoury flavour to dishes. Available in some major supermarkets as well as Asian supermarkets and online.

Hoisin sauce

Famously used with crispy duck pancakes, this thick, sweet and salty sauce is also an indispensable storecupboard ingredient used in stir-fries and sauces.

Lemongrass

These woody stalks add a delicate and aromatic lemony flavour to dishes. They can be frozen, so it's worth buying a few at a time – you can use it straight from the freezer.

Miso paste

A traditional Japanese fermented soya bean paste that gives an umami-packed depth of flavour to dishes, both savoury and sweet. There are several different types available, but for the purpose of these recipes I have used 'white miso'. You can also use products labelled just 'miso' (a light brown in colour and comparable in strength to white miso).

Noodles

I use rice, udon, egg, wheat, ready-to-wok and ramen. Most recipes will work with any type if you don't have the stated one to hand – just check the packet instructions so you know how to cook them.

Oyster sauce

A staple ingredient used in Thai and Chinese cooking, this adds a rounded saltiness to dishes.

Rice

My default is jasmine, which is used in Thai cuisine, as I love the stickier texture. However, basmati works just as well if that's what you have at home. I have given alternative quantities wherever possible.

Rice vinegar

Slightly sweeter and more delicate than other white vinegars. However, this can be substituted for white wine vinegar in most instances.

Sesame oil

Gives a nuttiness to dishes. Toasted sesame oil has a more pronounced flavour – if you can get it, that would always be my preference.

Sichuan peppercorns

A key spice used in Sichuan cuisine, which produces a slight tingling, numbing effect when eaten. Bought as whole peppercorns, it is best ground using a pestle and mortar, as needed.

Soy sauce

I use light soy sauce in these recipes. Interchange tamari for a gluten-free version.

Sriracha

A fermented Thai hot chilli sauce, used for dipping, drizzling and as a cooking ingredient. Adds heat, slight sweetness and a garlicky note to dishes.

Sweet chilli sauce

Perfect for adding instant sweetness and light heat to stir-fries and sauces. Use shop-bought or my Quick sweet chilli dipping sauce (page 188), which is also ideal for drizzling and dipping.

Tahini

A ground sesame paste that adds a lovely texture and nutty flavour.

Tamarind paste

This comes from the fruit of the tamarind tree and adds a sweet-tart flavour. You can buy it in tubs and jars and there are two types available – a brown variety (which is the one I use – see photo on page 13), and a tar-like, inky black version, which is far more concentrated. Both can be labelled as either tamarind paste or tamarind concentrate, making it hard to decipher which one to buy, so please assess based on colour and texture. If you can only get hold of the more concentrated version, simply use a third of the amount called for, and make up the rest of the amount with water, i.e. 1 tbsp tamarind paste = 1 tsp 'black' tamarind concentrate + 2 tsp water.

Thai curry paste

I would highly recommend buying a good-quality Thai brand paste such as Mae Ploy, available from some major supermarkets, all Asian shops and online (for a vegan option, I'd recommend Thai Taste). The flavour is far superior. If you're unable to get hold of a good one, then be sure to taste the dish as you go – you may need to add more paste and/or seasoning and chilli to compensate.

Tofu

Most of the tofu recipes in this book call for extra-firm tofu, which is perfect for stir-frying. Available in the chilled aisles. Silken tofu is soft and silky in texture and fragile to handle, and is also available widely, usually not chilled.

Wasabi paste

A green horseradish-like paste, usually served alongside plates of sushi. In this book I have put it to use as a salad dressing base. I use a shop-bought tube, which although it has some heat is far less potent than the fresh variety.

Key Kit

———

I've tried to keep kitchen equipment to a minimum but here are some key bits of kit that I couldn't live without.

Julienne peeler

This cuts vegetables like carrots and courgettes into lovely thin strips.

Chef's knife

A large, sharp chef's knife for meat and chopping veg. This doesn't have to be expensive. If you aren't used to one of these, don't be scared – with practice, using it will become second nature and will help make light work of your kitchen prep. It has to be sharp, though, so think about investing in a sharpening steel or a knife sharpener. You can use a smaller knife for more dainty tasks, like slicing an apple.

Fine grater

E.g. Microplane. Essential for ginger. Much more effective than a normal grater.

Garlic press

These recipes use a lot of garlic! This gadget will make your life a lot easier.

Measuring spoons

I use these when I'm cooking. No more guesstimating quantities with dubiously heaped spoonfuls! They will help ensure your measurements are as accurate as possible.

Non-stick pan

A large non-stick frying pan or wok is essential if you want an easy life!

Tips For Using The Recipes

Read the recipe

This might seem completely obvious, but my top tip would be: read the whole
recipe before you start cooking. I am entirely guilty of not always doing this myself,
so I speak from experience when I say *it will make your life a lot easier*
and will make the cooking process far more seamless.

Prep your ingredients

You'll see I put most of the prep in the ingredients list. It helps to get all the
ingredients you need out first, so you're not running around like a headless chicken
as you cook. Most of my recipes are so quick to cook that I find it's easiest to have
everything prepped and ready to go.

Taste, taste, taste

I can't stress this enough. Cooking and flavour is all down to individual preference.
Taste and adjust as you go. If you like it slightly saltier, add a pinch of salt or half a
teaspoon more soy sauce. My recipe is just the starting point. Start off slow, as you
can always add more but once it's in there, you can't take it away.

Flex your veg

Feel free to use different veg, depending on what you have and what's in season. In
most cases, the recipes are flexible. Just try to use approximately the same amount
and adjust cooking times accordingly.

Small Plates
& Nibbles

One-Bite Prawn Wraps

Preparation time: 15 minutes

Cooking time: 10 minutes

Serves 4 as a starter

—

For the sauce

1 tbsp unsweetened crunchy
    peanut butter

50ml water

4 tbsp soft brown sugar

2 tbsp tamarind paste
    (see note, page 15)

2 tbsp fish sauce

1 tsp grated ginger (approx. 2cm)

½ tsp dried red chilli flakes
    (optional)

To serve

16 large spinach, little gem
    or betel leaves

16 cooked peeled king prawns

1 lime, cut into wedges

3 tbsp desiccated coconut, toasted

4 tbsp salted peanuts, roughly
    chopped

¼ of a red onion, finely chopped

I stumbled across these prawn wraps – full name miang kham, meaning 'one bite wrap' – in London restaurant Farang a few years ago, and I have been dreaming of them ever since.

These playful little morsels are everything you could possibly want in one bite – a combination of different textures and flavours that disco-dance in your mouth, making them utterly irresistible. Crunchy, crispy, sticky – not to mention spicy, salty, sour and sweet – miang has it all. My simplified version is surprisingly easy to make – just try not to eat them all before your guests arrive.

Note: *This dish is traditionally made with betel leaves; however, large spinach leaves (big enough to wrap a prawn in, but not the giant variety) or little gem leaves work just as well.*

———————————

Place the peanut butter in a small pan and slowly mix in the water to make a smooth paste (bits of peanut aside). Place over a medium heat, stir in the other sauce ingredients and simmer for a few minutes, stirring occasionally, until the sauce thickens and reduces by about half. Remove from the heat and leave to cool.

To assemble, place the leaves on a serving plate. Top each one with a prawn, a drizzle of sauce and a light squeeze of lime, followed by a sprinkling of coconut, peanuts and red onion.

Alternatively, lay out all the elements in small dishes, and let your guests assemble their miang themselves.

Teriyaki Chicken Puffs

Preparation time: 25 minutes

Cooking time: 20–25 minutes

Makes 8

—

1 x 320g pack of ready-rolled
   puff pastry

½ tsp cornflour

1 tbsp water

2 tbsp light soy sauce

2 tbsp mirin

1 tbsp caster sugar

neutral oil, for frying

2 spring onions, finely sliced

1 clove of garlic, crushed

1 large chicken breast (200g),
   cut into 1cm cubes

1 egg, lightly beaten

These irresistible parcels will put a smile on your face. I'm a sucker for puff pastry, and when you add a tantalizing savoury-sweet filling of teriyaki chicken, you really can't go wrong. It takes just minutes to put the filling together, and while there is a bit of preparation in assembling the parcels, it's all pretty straightforward once you get into your stride.

These are perfect for drinks parties or entertaining, snacks with friends or a light bite, and will go down an absolute storm.

———————

Line a baking tray and preheat the oven to 200°C/180°C fan/gas mark 6.

Remove the puff pastry from the fridge, ready to use.

To make the sauce, mix the cornflour with the water in a small bowl, then stir in the soy sauce, mirin and sugar. Set near the stove.

Heat 1 tablespoon of oil in a frying pan over a medium heat. Add the spring onions and garlic and cook for 1 minute, stirring constantly. Add the chicken and cook for about 2 minutes, until cooked. Pour in the sauce and bubble gently for a couple of minutes, until it thickens and reduces enough to coat the chicken – you don't want any excess liquid.

Remove the chicken mixture from the pan and spread out on a plate to cool.

Unroll the puff pastry and divide it into 8 equal-sized rectangles, then transfer to the lined tray. Divide the cooled filling between the pastry rectangles, placing it on one half of each piece, leaving a border. Brush the border with a little egg and fold over each rectangle, first sealing with your fingers, then using a fork to crimp the edges. Make sure there are no gaps.

Brush each one with more egg and bake in the oven for 15–20 minutes, until golden brown on top. Delicious served warm.

Thai Tuna Fishcakes

Preparation time: 15 minutes

Cooking time: 10 minutes

Makes approximately 10 fish cakes

Serves 3-4 as a starter

—

2 x 145g tins of tuna, drained

1 egg, lightly beaten

1½ tbsp Thai red curry paste

3 tbsp cornflour

1 spring onion, finely sliced

1 tbsp neutral oil, for frying

To serve

squeeze of lime

Quick sweet chilli dipping sauce – page 188

Thai fish cakes (tod mun pla) are a classic Thai dish, just as popular here as they are in Thailand. The traditional recipe uses white fish fillets, but I have used tinned tuna instead for an easy storecupboard fix. The results are just as impressive and I'm pleased to say they got a big thumbs-up from my mum!

Note: *I use Mae Ploy Thai red curry paste, which gives the fishcakes good depth of flavour. If you're unable to get hold of any, you'll need to do a taste test and add more paste, as necessary.*

———

Place everything apart from the oil in a mixing bowl and mash well with a fork, making sure the curry paste is properly mixed through. Take a small teaspoon's worth of mixture – you can use this one to test the seasoning. Heat a drizzle of oil in a large non-stick frying pan and fry for a couple of minutes, or until cooked. Taste, and if it needs any salt or extra curry paste, add a little to the rest of the mixture.

Take heaped dessertspoons of the mixture and shape into patties.

Heat 1 tablespoon of oil in a large non-stick frying pan over a medium heat. Add the patties and fry for around 2–3 minutes on each side, until golden. Place on kitchen paper to drain off any excess oil.

Serve immediately, with a squeeze of lime. Perfect dipped in sweet chilli sauce or teamed with my Cucumber relish (page 183).

Crispy Broccoli
with Spicy Peanut Sauce

Preparation time: 10 minutes

Cooking time: 20–25 minutes

Serves 4

—

For the broccoli

1 head of broccoli

2 tbsp neutral oil

For the spicy peanut sauce

2 tbsp unsweetened crunchy
    peanut butter

1 tbsp crispy chilli oil, with bits

½–1 tsp honey (or to taste)

½–1 tsp light soy sauce (or to taste)

Broccoli remains one of my favourite vegetables, usually just charred for a few minutes in a frying pan with a pinch of sea salt flakes. However, intrigued by an Instagram trend for crispy baked broccoli, I decided to experiment. This method of cooking is hassle-free and results in the most incredible dish – so, so simple, but before you know it you've munched a whole tray 'just to test if it's cooked'. Even my kids can't keep their hands off. Pair it with a spicy peanut sauce and you have something amazing.

Note: *This recipe calls for a crispy chilli oil with bits, not just plain chilli oil. The heat and salt levels vary from brand to brand, so you need to start slowly with the honey and soy sauce and adjust according to personal preference.*

Preheat the oven to 220°C/200°C fan/gas mark 7.

Cut the broccoli into small florets and the stalks into long, thin pieces. Place on a large roasting tray, drizzle over the oil, add a good sprinkling of sea salt and toss to coat. Cook in the oven for 20–25 minutes, or until the florets are crispy and a little charred.

Meanwhile, make the sauce. Combine the ingredients together in a small bowl. Start with the smallest amount of both honey and soy sauce and adjust according to taste. Add a tablespoon or two of water to loosen – you're looking for a sauce with a drizzling consistency, so you may need to add a little more.

Serve the broccoli hot out of the oven, drizzled with the sauce.

Sweet Potato & Spring Onion Fritters

Preparation time: 15 minutes

Cooking time: 15 minutes

Makes 12–14 fritters

Serves 4–6

—

For the fritters

1 large sweet potato (approx. 300g), peeled and grated

75g plain flour

2 tbsp cornflour

2 spring onions, finely sliced

½ tsp fine salt

neutral oil, for frying

To serve

6 tbsp mayonnaise

2 tsp gochujang paste or sriracha

These four-ingredient fritters are so simple and completely irresistible. Perfect as a starter or for a drinks party.

Note: *If you don't have spring onions, a little finely chopped white or red onion would work well in their place.*

———————

Place all the ingredients for the fritters, apart from the oil, in a mixing bowl and combine well. Use your hands to squeeze the mixture into small patties, as flat as possible, about a heaped dessertspoon's worth each. The mixture will feel dry, but you'll find it's easy to scrunch it together.

Heat 2 tablespoons of oil in a large non-stick frying pan over a medium heat. Once hot, add the patties and fry for around 2–3 minutes on each side, until crispy and golden brown. Place on kitchen paper to drain off any excess oil. You may have to cook them in batches.

Mix the mayo with the gochujang or sriracha and serve with the warm fritters.

Steamed Tofu
with Oyster Sauce

Preparation time: 10 minutes

Cooking time: 5–10 minutes

Serves 2

—

2 tbsp oyster sauce

1 tbsp light soy sauce

1 tbsp caster sugar

1 tbsp rice vinegar

3 tbsp water

1 x 300g block of silken tofu

neutral oil, for frying

1 clove of garlic, crushed

1 tsp grated ginger (approx. 2cm)

2 spring onions, finely sliced

This steamed tofu dish is a complete joy, soft and delicate, yet full of flavour, thanks to the delicious garlic, ginger, spring onion and oyster sauce. I served it to my family, expecting the kids to leave it – but to my surprise, they scoffed the lot and asked for more!

————————

Mix the oyster sauce, soy sauce, sugar, rice vinegar and water together and place near a stove.

Carefully slide the tofu on to a small serving plate with a rim, leave for a minute, then dab the plate with kitchen paper to remove any excess water.

Steam the tofu. To do this in a microwave, cover and heat on medium for 2 minutes, or until warm. Alternatively, place the plate in a steamer over a pan of simmering water and steam for 6–8 minutes. Carefully drain away any excess liquid. Cut the tofu into 2cm slices on the serving plate.

Heat 1 teaspoon of oil in a small frying pan over a medium heat. Add the garlic, ginger and spring onions and stir-fry for 1 minute. Turn the heat down slightly and add the sauce. Simmer for 1 minute until thickened slightly.

Pour the sauce over the tofu and serve.

Clockwise from top left: Korean-style pork lettuce cups (page 39), Teriyaki chicken puffs (page 22), Quick sweet chilli dipping sauce (page 188), Prawn cakes (page 35), Quick cucumber pickle (page 183).

Prawn Cakes

Preparation time: 10 minutes

Cooking time: 10 minutes

Makes 8–9 patties

Serves 3–4

—

300g raw peeled prawns

2 cloves of garlic, crushed

2 tsp Thai green curry paste

zest of 1 lime

2–3 tbsp cornflour, for dusting

neutral oil, for frying

To serve

lime wedges

Quick sweet chilli dipping sauce –
    page 188

If I had to choose a desert island meal, prawns would definitely make the list. They feature heavily in Thai cuisine, and when we were children my mum fed them to us regularly, most often boiled and dipped in sweet chilli.

I came up with these easy prawn cakes one evening when Mum was over for dinner and they went down a storm. The kids devoured them too, so it's fair to say they were a success. Feel free to double the quantities if feeding a group – I promise they won't last long!

Note: *The salt in curry pastes can vary quite significantly, so it is worth doing a small test before you fry the whole batch.*

———————

Place the prawns, garlic, curry paste and lime zest in a food processor and pulse until everything is chopped but still has some texture.

Sprinkle the cornflour on a large plate. Take a small teaspoon's worth of mixture and roll it in the flour – you can use this one to test the seasoning. Heat a drizzle of oil in a large non-stick frying pan and fry for a couple of minutes, or until cooked. Taste, and if it needs any salt, add a pinch or two to the rest of the mixture.

Make small patties, approximately a heaped dessertspoon's worth each, with the rest of the mixture, then coat them in the cornflour.

Heat a further tablespoon of oil in the frying pan over a medium heat and add the patties to the pan.

Fry for 3–4 minutes on each side, until golden and cooked through. Place on kitchen paper to drain off any excess oil. Serve immediately, with a squeeze of lime and a drizzle of sweet chilli sauce.

Two Nuts to Nibble

5-Spice Roasted Peanuts

Preparation time: 5 minutes

Cooking time: 18 minutes

Serves 4

—

200g raw peanuts

1 tbsp neutral oil

½ tsp fine salt

2 tsp Chinese 5-spice

½ tsp chilli powder

1 tbsp soft brown sugar

Preheat the oven to 190°C/170°C fan/gas mark 5.

Place all the ingredients in a bowl and mix, making sure the peanuts are evenly coated.

Pour on to a baking sheet and cook for 12–18 minutes, or until golden brown. Cool and serve.

Will keep for 3 days in an airtight container.

Black Pepper & Chilli Cashews

Preparation time: 5 minutes

Cooking time: 12 minutes

Serves 4

—

200g raw cashew nuts

1 tbsp neutral oil

½ tsp fine salt

2 tsp soft brown sugar

1 tsp chilli powder (use less if you prefer a milder heat)

1 tsp finely ground black pepper

Preheat the oven to 190°C/170°C fan/gas mark 5.

Place all the ingredients in a bowl and mix, making sure the cashews are evenly coated.

Pour on to a baking sheet and cook for 10–12 minutes, or until the cashews are golden brown. Cool and serve.

Will keep for 3 days in an airtight container.

Korean-Style Pork Lettuce Cups

Preparation time: 10 minutes

Cooking time: 10 minutes

Serves 4

—

For the sauce

1 tbsp gochujang paste

1 tbsp light soy sauce

1 tbsp honey

For the pork

neutral oil, for frying

2 spring onions, finely sliced

2 cloves of garlic, crushed

250g pork mince, ideally over 10% fat content

To serve

2 little gem lettuces, or similar

30g salted peanuts, chopped

2 spring onions, finely sliced

lime wedges (optional)

red chilli, finely sliced (optional)

Quick cucumber pickle – page 183

Spicy and well-balanced, these lettuce cups combine many flavours I love – a bit of chilli heat from the gochujang, salty crunch from the peanuts and sweet and sour from the cucumber pickle. Ready in around 20 minutes, this is a fab dish any day of the week but is great for serving to guests, too. The garnishes and pork can be prepared and cooked in advance – simply reheat the pork when you're ready.

Note: *Any leftover mince is delicious served with rice and a fried egg.*

In a small bowl, combine the ingredients for the sauce and place near the stove.

Heat 1 tablespoon of oil in a large frying pan or wok over a medium-high heat. Add the spring onions and garlic and stir-fry for 1 minute or so, until softened.

Turn the heat up and add the pork mince. Stir-fry for a few minutes, until browned, breaking up the meat as you go.

Reduce the heat to medium, add the sauce and combine well. Cook for a further 2 minutes, then taste – if you like more spice, stir through another teaspoon or so of gochujang paste. Turn off the heat.

Place the pork in a serving dish, alongside the lettuce and other garnishes. Allow people to assemble their lettuce cups themselves.

Salads

Thai Crispy Rice Salad

Preparation time: 15 minutes

**Cooking time: 15 minutes
(plus rice cooking)**

**Serves 2 as a starter or
as part of a larger meal**

—

200g cooked jasmine rice, cooled
(approx. 80g uncooked weight of
jasmine or basmati rice)

½ tbsp Thai red curry paste

3 tbsp cornflour

2 tbsp neutral oil, for frying

For the dressing

3 tbsp lime juice (approx. 2 limes)

2 tbsp soft brown sugar

1½ tbsp fish sauce

1 red chilli (use bird's-eye if you
like it hot), finely chopped

For the salad

½ a small red onion, very thinly
sliced

a small handful of mint leaves,
shredded

a small handful of coriander,
shredded

50g salted peanuts, roughly
chopped

Walking through the doors of Supawan restaurant in King's Cross, we were greeted with the unmistakable waft of Thailand – a familiar warm pungency, the smell of fish sauce, of curry pastes frying and umami in the air. Reading the southern Thai menu, I felt giddy with excitement – and I'm delighted to say the food more than delivered its promise.

Their crispy rice salad – or yum khao tod – was so good we ordered seconds, and it is the inspiration behind this recipe. The rice is fried for a crispy, chewy texture, then combined with a zingy Thai dressing, herbs and crunchy peanuts. Simple but incredible.

Note: *As with any dish with chillies, taste and feel free to add more, if necessary!*

———————

Mix the rice with the curry paste and a good pinch of salt and combine well. Stir in the cornflour, ensuring each grain is coated.

Heat the oil in a large non-stick frying pan over a medium heat. Add the rice in a thin layer and press down. Leave to cook for around 5–7 minutes, or until a golden crust forms. Gently turn over and repeat on the other side. You may need to add a drizzle more oil. It doesn't matter if it breaks up, but you do want to try and make sure you have as much crust as possible.

Remove the rice from the pan and leave to cool.

In the meantime, make the dressing. Combine all the ingredients, making sure the sugar is dissolved.

Put the rice into a large serving bowl and break any larger pieces into chunks. Pour over the dressing and mix through the salad ingredients. Eat immediately.

Hot Honey & Ginger Roasted Carrots with 5-Spice Cabbage

Preparation time: 20 minutes

Cooking time: 30–40 minutes

**Serves 2 for lunch
  or 4 as a side**

—

3 tbsp honey

1 tsp grated ginger (approx. 2cm)

½–1 tsp dried red chilli flakes
  (to taste)

400g carrots, cut into thick batons

½ a red cabbage, finely shredded

neutral oil

1 tsp Chinese 5-spice

75g natural yoghurt

a handful of coriander, roughly torn

2 tbsp pumpkin seeds or mixed
  seeds, toasted

This roasted salad may be a departure from the usual fresh and zesty variety, but the flavours really do shine and come together to make something quite special. The ginger and chilli-infused honey glaze intensifies the sweetness of the carrots, contrasting against the crispy, salty 5-spice-roasted cabbage. The seeds add crunch and the cooling yoghurt brings the plate together in harmony.

———————————

Preheat the oven to 220°C/200°C fan/gas mark 7.

Heat the honey, ginger and chilli flakes in a small saucepan over a low to medium heat for around 3 minutes, stirring occasionally. Once it starts to bubble, take the pan off the heat.

You will need two large roasting trays. Place the carrots in one, and the cabbage in the other. For the carrots, drizzle over ½ tablespoon of oil, along with a good pinch or two of sea salt flakes and half the hot honey mix. For the cabbage, drizzle over 1 tablespoon of oil, along with a good pinch or two of sea salt flakes and the Chinese 5-spice. Make sure both vegetables are well coated.

Put the carrots into the oven, then add the cabbage after 10 minutes. Cook for a further 20 minutes and check both trays. The carrots should be tender and caramelized. The cabbage should be cooked down and caramelized, with lots of crispy (but not burnt) bits. Put back into the oven for another 5–10 minutes if necessary.

Meanwhile, make the yoghurt dressing. Place the yoghurt in a small bowl and ripple through the remaining hot honey mix – you may need to slightly warm the honey if it has become too firm. Place in the fridge until needed.

To assemble, place the red cabbage on a serving dish, top with the coriander, carrots and toasted seeds, then drizzle over the yoghurt dressing.

Spicy Thai Mushroom Salad

Preparation time: 10 minutes

Cooking time: 8 minutes

Serves 2 as a starter or as part of a bigger meal

—

3 tbsp lime juice
  (approx. 2 limes)

1 tbsp fish sauce

1 tsp soft brown sugar

½ tsp dried red chilli flakes
  (or to taste)

neutral oil, for frying

250g chestnut or shiitake
  mushrooms, chopped into
  1–2cm pieces

2 cloves of garlic, crushed

½ a small red onion, finely sliced

a small handful of coriander,
  chopped

a small handful of mint leaves,
  chopped

This spicy mushroom salad is inspired by larb – a fiery salad from Laos and Thailand usually made with ground meat. The mushrooms are a delicious alternative and work brilliantly with the chilli-spiked, zingy dressing. A simple dish, but one that packs a punch.

—

First, make the dressing. Combine the lime, fish sauce, sugar and chilli flakes and set aside.

Heat 2 tablespoons of oil in a large frying pan over a medium-high heat. Add the mushrooms and a good pinch of salt and fry for 5 minutes, stirring occasionally. Add the garlic, and another drizzle of oil if necessary. Cook for another 2–3 minutes, or until the mushrooms are golden brown.

Place in a serving dish and spoon over the dressing – you may not need to add all of it, so start slowly. Mix through the remaining ingredients and serve immediately. Any leftover dressing would be great drizzled on a few cherry tomatoes for a quick side salad.

Seared Tuna & Wasabi Salad

Preparation time: 15 minutes

Cooking time: 7–8 minutes

Serves 2 as a light lunch

—

For the dressing

3 tbsp rice vinegar

3 tbsp neutral oil

1½ tsp light soy sauce

1½ tsp wasabi paste

¾ tsp caster sugar

For the salad

2 large eggs

neutral oil

2 x fresh tuna steaks
(approx. 100g each)

40g salad leaves

75g sugar snap peas,
thinly sliced lengthways

8 cherry tomatoes, halved

¼ of a medium cucumber,
cut into quarter slices

¼ of a red onion, thinly sliced

Over the years I must have eaten nearly every item on the menu of my local Japanese, Wow Simply Japanese in Crouch End. Of their many standout dishes, the tuna tartare with wasabi dressing has always been up there. That fantastic dressing was the starting point for this recipe, which then evolved into a tuna Niçoise-inspired salad. The seared tuna takes things up a notch – this would make a great weekend lunch.

Whisk the ingredients for the dressing in a small bowl and set aside.

Bring a small saucepan of water to the boil and add the eggs. Lower the heat slightly to a simmer. Cook the eggs for 6 minutes for soft-boiled or 7 minutes for a slightly jammier yolk. Remove immediately and run under cold water for a minute or so. Peel and cut in half.

Meanwhile, prepare the vegetables and assemble on a serving dish.

Heat a non-stick frying pan over a high heat. Drizzle 1 tablespoon of oil over both tuna steaks, and season well with sea salt flakes and black pepper. When the pan is very hot, add the steaks and cook for 30–45 seconds or so on each side, depending on thickness. You want them to be seared and browned on the outside, but rare in the middle. Leave to stand for a couple of minutes, then slice thinly.

Arrange the tuna and eggs over the salad and drizzle over a couple of spoonfuls of the dressing. Serve immediately, with the rest of the dressing on the side.

Thai Prawn & Pineapple Salad

Preparation time: 15–20 minutes

Serves 2 as a light lunch or more as part of a larger meal

—

For the dressing

3 tbsp lime juice (approx. 2 limes)

2 tbsp fish sauce

1½ tbsp soft brown sugar

½–1 tsp dried red chilli flakes (according to taste)

For the salad

4cm slice of fresh pineapple, peeled, cored and cut into small bite-sized pieces

100g white cabbage, thinly shredded (equivalent to a small wedge)

200g cooked peeled king prawns

¼ of a red onion, finely sliced

a handful of coriander, chopped

2 tbsp salted peanuts, roughly chopped

When I visit Thailand, barely a day goes by when I don't eat either prawns or pineapple in some capacity. Here they're united to create a little party on the plate with contrasting layers and textures – juicy prawns, sweet pineapple, salty nuts and crunchy cabbage – all brought together with herbs and a punchy Thai dressing.

————

Mix the ingredients for the dressing together in a small bowl, making sure the sugar dissolves. Set aside.

Put the pineapple, cabbage, prawns, red onion and coriander into a large bowl and pour over the dressing. Toss to combine, then spoon into a serving dish, if using. Sprinkle over the peanuts and eat immediately.

Zingy Apple
& Red Cabbage Salad

Preparation time: 15 minutes

Serves 2–4 as a side

—

For the dressing

2 tbsp lime juice
   (approx. 1 ½ limes)

1 tbsp fish sauce

1 tbsp soft brown sugar

½–1 tsp dried red chilli flakes
   (according to taste)

For the salad

1 apple, cut into matchsticks
   (Granny Smith or similar is ideal)

100g red cabbage, thinly shredded
   (equivalent to a small wedge)

¼ of a red onion, finely sliced

a small handful of coriander,
   chopped

a small handful of mint leaves,
   chopped

30g toasted hazelnuts, chopped

2 tbsp shop-bought crispy fried
   onions (optional)

One winter's evening, I had the urge for a plate of fresh and fiery som tam – one of my top Thai salads. I set about creating something with the ingredients I had to hand (sadly green papaya wasn't one of them!) and this salad is the result. A brilliantly zingy and vibrant dish that hits all the right notes – aromatic, spicy, sweet and sour, with lots of crunch. Delicious on its own, or served with meat dishes such as my Crispy chicken wings (page 69) or Cumin-spiced lamb flatbreads (page 78).

———————

Mix the ingredients for the dressing together in a small bowl, making sure the sugar dissolves. Set aside.

Place the apple, red cabbage, onion, coriander and mint in a large bowl and pour over the dressing. Combine, then tip into a serving dish, if using. Sprinkle over the hazelnuts and the crispy fried onions, if using, and eat immediately.

Prawn Ramen Noodle Salad

Preparation time: 15 minutes

Cooking time: 2–4 minutes

Serves 2 as a light lunch

—

For the dressing

2 tbsp lime juice
(approx 1½ limes)

2 tbsp tamarind paste
(see note, page 15)

2 tsp fish sauce

2 tsp soft brown sugar

1 tsp dried red chilli flakes
(or to taste)

For the noodles

1 portion of ramen noodles

150g cooked peeled prawns

1 carrot, shredded with a julienne
peeler or cut into matchsticks

100g green veg, e.g. sugar snap
peas, mangetout, courgettes, cut
into thin strips or matchsticks

a handful of mint leaves, chopped

a handful of coriander, chopped

The desire for sunny food can hit me just as easily on a winter's day as it does in midsummer, when all I want is a plate of something light and vibrant to energize my body and my tastebuds. This prawn noodle salad does just that. My auntie used to make a gorgeous one with glass noodles, which inspired this version. Here I have used tamarind in the dressing, for added sour tanginess.

—————————————

Cook the noodles according to the packet instructions. Drain and rinse.

Combine the ingredients for the dressing in a small bowl, making sure the sugar dissolves.

Place the noodles, prawns and veg in a mixing bowl and pour over the dressing. Combine. Add the mint and coriander and gently toss, then divide between two bowls and serve immediately.

Asian-Style Slaw

Preparation time: 25 minutes

Serves 4–6 as a side

—

200g white cabbage,
    finely shredded

2 large carrots, shredded with a
    julienne peeler or grated

½ a medium red onion, finely sliced

50g salted peanuts, chopped

a large handful of coriander,
    chopped

a large handful of mint leaves,
    chopped

For the dressing

1 clove of garlic, crushed

1 red chilli, finely chopped

4 tbsp lime juice (about 2–3 limes)

2 tbsp caster sugar

2 tbsp fish sauce

2 tsp rice vinegar

Crunchy, spicy, zingy, herby – this slaw has it all. I often crave it when I want something healthy but packed full of flavour. It also works well as a light lunch (you could throw in some prawns if you wanted). Adding vibrancy to a meal, the freshness complements an array of Asian dishes, particularly barbecued or griddled meats and fish.

———————

Combine the ingredients for the dressing in a small bowl and stir, making sure the sugar is dissolved.

Put the cabbage, carrot and onion into a large bowl. Pour in the dressing and toss well.

Place the slaw in a serving dish, if using. Mix in the peanuts, coriander and mint, and eat immediately.

Hot Smoked Salmon Rice Bowl with Miso Dressing

Preparation time: 10 minutes (plus rice cooking)

Serves 2 as a light lunch

—

For the dressing

2 tbsp rice vinegar

2 tbsp neutral oil

1 tbsp miso or white miso

¾ tsp Dijon mustard

1½–2 tsp caster sugar (to taste)

1 tsp water

For the rice bowl

250g cooked rice (approx. 110g uncooked weight of jasmine rice, 90g if using basmati)

150–200g hot-smoked salmon

1 ripe avocado, sliced

5–6 radishes, thinly sliced

100g cooked edamame beans

1 spring onion, finely sliced

Rich, salty and slightly sweet, hot smoked salmon is a wonderful lunchtime ingredient, particularly when you want something quick but intensely flavoured. I often have it with cream cheese or crab pâté on a bagel, with a drizzle of my Quick sweet chilli dipping sauce (page 188), or in place of the seared tuna in my Niçoise–inspired salad (page 48).

In this dish, the smokiness of the salmon perfectly complements the creamy avocado and edamame beans, while the radishes bring welcome freshness and crunch. The tangy, sharp dressing brings all the components together, making this tasty bowl a regular on my lunch menu. Smoked mackerel would make a great alternative.

———————

Whisk the ingredients for the dressing in a bowl and set aside.

Divide the rice between two bowls, then top with the rest of the rice bowl ingredients. Drizzle over the dressing and serve.

Oven &
Grill Dishes

———

Tamarind, Honey & Sesame Chicken

Preparation time: 15 minutes, plus 20 minutes optional marinating time

Cooking time: 50 minutes

Serves 4

—

120g tamarind paste

8 tbsp honey

3 tbsp fish sauce

2 tbsp light soy sauce

2 tbsp sesame oil, preferably toasted

4 cloves of garlic, crushed

½ tsp salt

4 spring onions, cut into 5cm pieces

8 chicken thighs, skin on, bone in, fat trimmed

To serve

spring onion, finely sliced

Delicious served with

rice

Quick cucumber pickle – page 183

Garlicky green beans – page 168

Peanut serundeng – page 163

I first discovered the joys of tamarind a few years ago when my Thai auntie Dang brought us a jar of her homemade tamarind sauce. It was a complete revelation, and after one taste I was hooked. Made from just tamarind, fish sauce and sugar, it was sticky and sweet, and the perfect match for our crispy fried salmon that night. Since then tamarind has become a much loved ingredient of mine, and the combination here with honey, garlic and sesame oil, on juicy chicken thighs, borders on the addictive.

Note: *I use the brown variety of tamarind. If you have the more concentrated, inky-black version, just use 40g here, loosened with 5 tablespoons of water.*

———————

Preheat the oven to 200°C/180°C fan/gas mark 6.

In a jug, combine the tamarind, honey, fish sauce, soy sauce, sesame oil, garlic and salt.

Pour half the sauce into a roasting tray, then add the spring onions. Score each chicken thigh twice, then place on top, skin side up. Coat the flesh but leave the skin dry. Reserve the remaining sauce for drizzling over the finished dish. If you have time, leave to marinate for at least 20 minutes – if not, proceed to the next step.

Sprinkle each chicken thigh with sea salt flakes and a touch of black pepper, then place in the oven for 40–50 minutes, or until cooked through. If you like a crispier skin, heat the grill to high and place the tray under it for a minute or two, or until the skin is done to your liking.

Once ready, sprinkle the chicken with thinly sliced spring onion. Combine the tray juices with the leftover sauce and drizzle over liberally. Great with bowls of rice, Cucumber pickle and Garlicky green beans, sprinkled with a few spoonfuls of Peanut serundeng.

Roasted Cauliflower
with Satay Sauce

Preparation time: 5–10 minutes

Cooking time: 30–40 minutes

Serves 2

—

1 head of cauliflower, cut into small bite-sized florets

2 tbsp neutral oil

2 tbsp curry powder

For the sauce

neutral oil

1½ tbsp Thai red curry paste

100ml coconut milk

5 tbsp unsweetened crunchy peanut butter

1–1½ tbsp soft brown sugar (according to taste)

1 tsp light soy sauce

75–100ml water

To serve

rice

coriander, chopped

red chillies, finely sliced (optional)

Plates of satay skewers piled high, bowlfuls of spicy peanut sauce on the side, and a pot of steaming rice. This is what dinner often looked like when I was a child – how lucky we were! In this recipe, spice-roasted cauliflower is enrobed in my mum's luscious peanut sauce, taking the dish in an almost curry-like direction. A mouth-watering, outrageously good meal.

Note: *Curry pastes can vary wildly in terms of heat and salt levels, so it's important to taste and adjust the seasoning as you go.*

Preheat the oven to 240°C/220°C fan/gas mark 9.

Place the cauliflower on a large baking tray. Drizzle over the 2 tablespoons of oil and sprinkle over a couple of pinches of sea salt flakes and the curry powder. Toss to coat and combine well.

Roast in the oven for 25 minutes, or until golden, tender and beginning to caramelize, tossing halfway.

Meanwhile, make the sauce. Heat 1 teaspoon of oil in a small pan over a low to medium heat. Add the curry paste and fry for 1 minute or so, until aromatic. Slowly stir in the coconut milk, then add the peanut butter, 1 tablespoon of the sugar, the soy sauce and 75ml of water. The sauce should be thick enough to coat the cauliflower, but feel free to add a little more water if you prefer it slightly thinner. Taste the sauce and add extra sugar or a pinch of salt, if needed.

Spoon the warm sauce over the roasted cauliflower and serve with rice, coriander and chillies, if desired.

Crispy Chicken Wings
with Spicy BBQ Sauce

Preparation time: 10 minutes

Cooking time: 30–40 minutes

Serves 4

—

2 tsp baking powder

½ tsp fine salt

1kg chicken wings

For the sauce

4 tbsp tomato ketchup

4 tbsp hoisin sauce

2 tbsp sriracha

2½ tsp honey

To serve

spring onion, finely sliced

Delicious served with

Zingy apple & red cabbage
 – page 54

I have one of my Woolf's Kitchen clients, David Reekie, to thank for these crispy beauties. He shared his secret of coating chicken wings with baking powder and salt before cooking, resulting in the crispiest of skins. The wings are then slathered in a spicy, sweet sauce for ultimate finger-licking potential. Be prepared for them to be demolished!

———————

Preheat the oven to 230°C/210°C fan/gas mark 8. Place a rack over a lined baking tray.

Combine the baking powder and salt. Place the chicken wings in a large dish and dry the skin with kitchen paper. Sprinkle over the baking powder and salt mix, making sure the chicken skin is coated.

Place the wings on the rack and cook in the oven for 30 minutes, or until the skin is golden and crispy.

To make the sauce, simply combine all the ingredients in a small bowl.

Once the chicken wings are cooked, pour over most of the sauce and toss to coat. Place any remaining sauce in a bowl for extra dipping at the table. Sprinkle the chicken with finely sliced spring onion and serve immediately.

Thai Green Curry
Chicken & Rice Traybake

Preparation time: 15 minutes

Cooking time: 1 hour

Serves 4

—

4 tbsp Thai green curry paste

300ml water

300ml coconut milk

2 tsp fish sauce

300g jasmine rice, rinsed well

6–8 chicken thighs (approx. 1kg),
    skin on, bone in, fat trimmed

200g edamame beans or peas,
    or a mix

To serve

100g natural yoghurt

2 tsp sweet chilli sauce

1 lime, cut into wedges

a handful of coriander, chopped

red chillies, finely sliced (optional)

Using Thai green curry paste as a flavour base, this easy, flavourful traybake only requires minor input once it goes into the oven. The squeeze of lime lifts the dish and the yoghurt drizzle brings it all together.

Note: *I use Mae Ploy Thai green curry paste (which is spicier than many others), but if you prefer it on the mild side, then add less. Curry pastes do vary in heat so taste and tweak as necessary. If using basmati rice you will need 280g of rice, 400ml of coconut milk and 250ml of water.*

Preheat the oven to 200°C/180°C fan/gas mark 6.

Put 2 tablespoons of the curry paste into a large roasting tray or oven dish (approx. 25cm x 35cm) and gradually mix in the water to loosen. Pour in the coconut milk, add the fish sauce and a couple of pinches of salt, and stir to combine (don't worry if the coconut milk is lumpy at this point, it will dissolve as it cooks), then mix in the rice.

Slash each chicken thigh twice, then coat with the remaining 2 tablespoons of curry paste. Sprinkle with a pinch of sea salt flakes, then place the chicken on top of the rice skin side up and cover the dish with foil.

Bake for 30 minutes, then discard the foil. Move the chicken to one side while you give the rice a stir, then replace the chicken. Bake for a further 15 minutes, then take the tray out of the oven and mix the edamame beans or peas into the rice. Return to the oven and cook for a further 15 minutes, or until the rice is done and the chicken is completely cooked through. Taste the rice – if you'd like more heat, move the chicken to one side and stir in extra curry paste, to taste (loosen with water first, if needed). Check the seasoning and adjust with salt or fish sauce, if needed.

If you like a crispier skin, turn the grill to high and grill the whole dish for a minute or two, or until the skin is crispy. Put the yoghurt into a small bowl and stir in the sweet chilli sauce.

Serve with wedges of lime, sprinkled with chopped coriander and chillies, and with the yoghurt at the table for drizzling.

Lemongrass Lamb Chops

Preparation time: 10 minutes, plus marinating

Cooking time: 15 minutes

Serves 4

—

3 stalks of lemongrass

4 tbsp fish sauce

1 tsp ground turmeric

5 cloves of garlic, crushed

2½ tbsp soft brown sugar

2 tbsp sesame oil, preferably toasted

1 tsp dried red chilli flakes

8 lamb cutlets

neutral oil, for frying

For the nuoc cham

5 tsp caster sugar

2 tsp rice vinegar

4 tbsp water

1 small clove of garlic, crushed

½–1 red chilli, finely chopped (deseed for a milder heat)

1 tsp lime juice (about ½ a lime)

2 tbsp fish sauce

Delicious served with

Turmeric rice – page 175

Asian-style slaw – page 58

Charred corn with spring onion butter – page 170

These Vietnamese-inspired sizzling lamb chops make a wonderful weekend feast. The aromatic lemongrass marinade is a perfect match for the richness of the lamb, the smell of which while cooking is just heavenly. There's a riot of flavour going on, especially with the addition of nuoc cham, a spicy, salty, sweet-sour Vietnamese dipping sauce. This version, based on a recipe given to me by my Chinese-Vietnamese friend Amy La, is well balanced without being overpowering, allowing the lamb to shine.

Prepare the lemongrass. Remove the tough outer leaves and trim off the top ends. Bash them with the end of a rolling pin, then chop the inner leaves as finely as possible and place in a bowl. Add the remaining ingredients apart from the lamb and the neutral oil, and combine to make a marinade. Place the lamb chops in the bowl, coating each chop well in the marinade. Cover and leave for at least 30 minutes or overnight – the longer the better.

If marinating for longer, place in the fridge, being sure to remove an hour before cooking in order to bring the chops back up to room temperature.

To make the nuoc cham, heat the sugar, vinegar and water in a small pan over a medium heat until the sugar dissolves. Just before it comes to the boil, turn off the heat. Allow to cool slightly before adding the other ingredients. Combine and set aside until needed.

To cook the lamb chops, wipe away any excess marinade and season each side with sea salt flakes. Place the lamb chops closely together on their sides, fat side down, in a cold, large non-stick frying pan or griddle pan. You may need to do this in batches, depending on the size of your pan.

Turn the heat to medium-high and cook for 5–10 minutes, until the fat has rendered and become golden. Turn the chops over and cook for 2–3 minutes on each side, or until done to your liking. Leave to rest for 5 minutes.

Serve on a platter, with the nuoc cham dipping sauce on the side.

Chicken Satay Sandwich

Preparation time: 30 minutes

Cooking time: 20–25 minutes

Serves 4

—

For the chicken

100ml coconut milk

½ tsp each ground turmeric, cumin, coriander

2 large chicken breasts

For the satay sauce

neutral oil, for frying

1½ tbsp Thai red curry paste

100ml coconut milk

5 tbsp unsweetened crunchy peanut butter

1–1½ tbsp soft brown sugar (according to taste)

1 tsp light soy sauce

100ml water

For the pickles

150ml rice vinegar

1 tbsp sugar

¼ tsp fine salt

2 carrots, shredded with a julienne peeler or cut into matchsticks

200g white cabbage, finely shredded

To serve

4 small baguettes

a large handful or two of coriander

My mum's satay sauce is so good that I couldn't resist featuring it twice. It works brilliantly with my Roasted cauliflower (page 66), and here it's paired with chicken, the type of satay I grew up with, in an epic sandwich. Inspired by the concept of a banh mi, we have coconut-marinated chicken, vinegary pickles and aromatic coriander – all encased in an addictive spicy, nutty sauce. Yes, there are a few elements, so it does take a bit longer than usual, but if you're looking for an impressive lazy weekend brunch, you'll love this.

———————————

Place the coconut milk, turmeric, cumin and coriander in a dish and combine. Remove 1 tablespoon of this marinade and set aside for basting.

Place the chicken breasts on a board and cover with clingfilm. Using a rolling pin or a mallet, bash and flatten the chicken breasts evenly to around 1cm thick. Place the chicken in the marinade, add a pinch of salt, then cover and set aside while you make the rest of the dish.

To make the satay sauce, heat 1 teaspoon of oil in a small pan over a low to medium heat. Add the curry paste and fry for 30 seconds or so, until aromatic. Slowly stir in the coconut milk, then add the peanut butter, 1 tablespoon of the sugar, the soy sauce and the water. Taste the sauce and add extra sugar or a pinch of salt, if needed. Set aside to cool.

To make the pickles, put the vinegar, sugar and salt into a mixing bowl and stir to dissolve. Add the veg and combine well. Leave for at least 15 minutes.

Heat the grill on high and place the chicken breasts on a baking tray lined with foil. Grill for approximately 4–5 minutes on each side, or until cooked through. Let them sit for a couple of minutes, then slice thinly.

To serve, cut each baguette lengthways. Spoon in a little satay sauce, then top with chicken, more sauce, the pickles and some coriander.

Serve the remaining sauce and pickles on the table for people to help themselves.

Sticky Salmon Noodle Traybake

Preparation time: 10 minutes

Cooking time: 20 minutes

Serves 2

—

For the sauce

6 tbsp sweet chilli sauce

3 tbsp oyster sauce

1 tbsp light soy sauce

For the traybake

2 fillets of salmon, skin on

2 portions of pre-cooked medium egg or wheat noodles

1 carrot, cut into thin batons

1 tbsp sesame oil, preferably toasted

100g sugar snap peas

To serve

a small handful of coriander, chopped

1 red chilli, finely sliced (optional)

½ a lime, cut into wedges

If you're in need of a night off the wok, this all-in-one noodle bake is for you. I confess this is a bit of a cheat's sauce but it minimizes the chopping and hands-on work, giving you time for a leisurely kitchen clear-up while the oven does its thing. The noodles become delightfully crispy in places and the sweet chilli in the sauce works beautifully with the salmon. An easy, tasty dinner for those days when you don't fancy 'cooking'.

Note: *This will also work in an oven dish, but you may not have as many crispy noodle bits! Feel free to use dried noodles if that's what you have – simply cook them while you make the sauce, then rinse and drain.*

———————

Preheat the oven to 200°C/180°C fan/gas mark 6.

Mix the sauce ingredients together in a bowl, reserving 2 tablespoons for later. Add the salmon and coat.

Tip the noodles into a roasting tray or oven dish and spread out. Add the carrot, then drizzle over the sesame oil and toss to coat. Place in the oven for 5 minutes.

Remove the tray, add the sugar snap peas and pour the marinade from the salmon over the noodles. Mix through, then place the salmon on top. If the salmon has skin, scrape off any excess marinade and sprinkle with sea salt flakes. Return the tray to the oven for 15 minutes, or until the salmon is cooked.

Drizzle the reserved sauce over the noodles, combine, and serve sprinkled with the coriander and chilli, if desired, with lime wedges on the side.

Cumin-Spiced Lamb Flatbreads

Preparation time: 15 minutes

Cooking time: 25 minutes

Makes 6 flatbreads

—

neutral oil, for frying

1 onion, thinly sliced

3 cloves of garlic, crushed

250g lamb mince

1 tsp ground coriander

2 tsp ground cumin

1 tsp sugar

1 tsp dried red chilli flakes

1 tsp Sichuan peppercorns, ground

1 tsp grated ginger (approx. 2cm)

2 tsp light soy sauce

1 tbsp tomato purée

6 tortilla wraps (22cm diameter)

To serve

a small handful of coriander, roughly torn

spring onions, finely sliced

cherry tomatoes, halved

Rich and warmly spiced, these flatbreads borrow flavours from 'cumin lamb' – a classic dish from Xinjiang in north-west China, which uses cumin, chilli and Sichuan peppercorns. Bold yet beautifully balanced, the lamb works brilliantly when baked on flatbreads – akin to the idea of a lahmacun. A taste sensation. Try serving with my Quick pickled garlic & ginger carrots (page 185) or Spicy pineapple pickle (page 189).

Note: *You will need at least two large baking sheets for this recipe (or as many as you can fit into your oven).*

Preheat the oven to 200°C/180°C fan/gas mark 6.

Heat 1 tablespoon of oil in a frying pan over a medium heat. Add the onion and fry for 3 minutes, stirring occasionally, then add the garlic and fry for another couple of minutes, or until starting to soften.

Tip the onions and garlic into a large mixing bowl along with a large pinch of salt and all the other ingredients, apart from the tortilla wraps. Combine well.

Divide the mixture between the tortillas and spread thinly, towards the edges. Place them on baking sheets and cook in the oven for 5 minutes, or until the meat is cooked. You will probably have to do this in batches, depending on the size of your oven.

Top with the coriander, spring onions and tomatoes, and serve immediately. I like it with my Spicy pineapple pickle (page 189) or Quick-pickled garlic & ginger carrots (page 185).

5-Spice Chicken Thighs with Crispy Skin & Hoisin Pancakes

Preparation time: 20 minutes

Cooking time: 45 minutes

**Serves 8 as a starter
or 4 as part of a larger meal**

—

2 tbsp light soy sauce

½ tbsp sesame oil, preferably
toasted

2 cloves of garlic, crushed

3 tsp Chinese 5-spice, plus extra
for sprinkling

8 chicken thighs, skin on, bone in

To serve

1 cucumber, cut into thin
matchsticks

a small bunch of spring onions,
shredded lengthways

16–24 Chinese pancakes

hoisin sauce

One Christmas Day when I was about twelve, we decided to forego the turkey in favour of a home-roasted duck and Chinese pancakes. I'm pretty sure there were no sides, but that didn't matter – my brother and I were on cloud nine. To this day, I'm still crazy about the dish and order it whenever I get the chance. These easy roasted chicken thighs make a great alternative, and the crispy chicken skin is the cherry on top. It might seem like an extra step, but the reward is well worth it!

Note: *If you can't find Chinese pancakes, use mini tortillas, or large tortillas cut into 16–20cm rounds.*

———————

Preheat the oven to 200°C/180°C fan/gas mark 6.

In a large baking dish mix the soy sauce, sesame oil, garlic and 2 teaspoons of Chinese 5-spice.

Trim the chicken of any loose skin and set it aside. Slash the remaining skin on each thigh a couple of times, then place flesh side down on top of the soy mixture, leaving the skin dry. Sprinkle with the remaining teaspoon of Chinese 5-spice along with a good pinch of sea salt flakes.

For the crispy skin you will need two baking trays – one that will fit on top of the other. Line the bottom baking tray with greaseproof paper. Place the reserved skin on the lined baking tray, flatten out, and sprinkle each piece with sea salt flakes and a little Chinese 5-spice. Cover with another sheet of greaseproof paper and put the second baking tray on top.

Place the dish of chicken thighs, along with the tray of chicken skin, in the oven. The chicken skin should take around 30 minutes to become golden and crisp. Remove from the oven and continue cooking the chicken thighs for a further 10–20 minutes. Once the chicken is cooked, heat the grill to high and grill for a couple of minutes or so to really crisp up the skin on top.

Shred the chicken from the bone. Cut the crispy skin into pieces and serve alongside. Place the cucumber, spring onions, pancakes and hoisin sauce on the table and allow people to help themselves.

On The Stove

Sticky Chilli Chicken

Preparation time: 15 minutes

Cooking time: 15–20 minutes

Serves 2–3

—

For the sauce

4 tbsp sweet chilli sauce

2 tbsp tomato ketchup

2 tbsp sriracha

1 tbsp rice or white wine vinegar

1 tbsp light soy sauce

3 tbsp water

For the chicken

2 chicken breasts, sliced as thinly as possible (approx. 3mm)

4 tbsp cornflour

1 tsp salt

For the stir-fry

neutral oil, for frying

1 onion, sliced

1 red pepper, thinly sliced

2 cloves of garlic, crushed

1 tbsp grated ginger (approx. 6cm)

To serve

rice

1 spring onion, finely sliced

Unapologetically sticky and sweet, yet well balanced with some sriracha heat in the background, this is pure fakeaway heaven. Inspired by crispy chilli beef, this slightly less naughty version has weekend written all over it. This might just be my husband's favourite dish.

Note: *If your chicken breast is quite thick, it's worth carefully cutting it through the middle to give you two thin flat pieces before slicing.*

———————

Mix the sauce ingredients together in a bowl. Set aside near the stove.

Place the chicken in a dish or mixing bowl and sprinkle over the cornflour and salt. Toss to coat, making sure every piece is separated out and well covered. Add more cornflour, if necessary.

Heat 2 tablespoons of oil in a large non-stick frying pan over a high heat. Once the oil is hot, add the chicken, separating the pieces out as much as possible. Fry until golden and crisp all over, approximately 5–7 minutes (leave the chicken without turning it for the first few minutes, to enable it to brown properly). You may need to do this in batches, depending on the size of your pan. Remove and drain on kitchen paper.

Wipe the pan clean, if necessary, and add another tablespoon of oil. Lower the heat to medium-high. Add the onion and red pepper and cook for 2–3 minutes, until softened, then add the garlic and ginger and fry for a minute or so. Pour in the sauce and bubble for 30–60 seconds, or until thickened.

Put the chicken back into the pan, coat well with the sauce, and cook for a further minute.

Serve with rice and sliced spring onions.

Thai Sweet & Sour Fish

Preparation time: 10 minutes

Cooking time: 20 minutes

Serves 2

—

For the sauce

2 tbsp white wine vinegar

2 tbsp fish sauce

4½ tbsp tomato ketchup

2½ tbsp sugar

For the fish

2 tbsp cornflour

2 fillets of firm skinless white fish
  (such as sustainable cod or hake)

For the stir-fry

neutral oil, for frying

½ an onion, cut into wedges

2 cloves of garlic, crushed

100g cherry tomatoes, whole

½ a red pepper, cut into strips

¼ of a cucumber, cut into quarters
  lengthways, then into bite-size
  pieces on the diagonal

2cm slice of pineapple, peeled,
  cored and cut into bite-sized
  pieces

To serve

rice

'No, no, that's not how we do it,' said my mum, shaking her head in dismay, when I told her my plans for her sweet and sour recipe. She always made it with prawns and occasionally chicken, but never with fillets of fish. Just not the done thing. I'm glad I persevered, because the resulting dish is a banger. Made with cherry tomatoes and peppers, the sauce is alive with fresh flavours and just the right amount of tangy sweetness.

Note: *Of course prawns are still delicious in this dish, so go ahead and swap them for the fish if you want. Simply add them after the onions and garlic.*

Mix the sauce ingredients together in a bowl and set aside.

Put the cornflour on a plate. Dry the fish well with kitchen paper, then coat it in the cornflour. Sprinkle a good pinch of sea salt flakes on each side.

Heat 2 tablespoons of oil in a large non-stick frying pan over a medium-high heat. Once it is very hot, add the fish, shaking off any excess flour, and fry for 2–3 minutes on the first side without touching, until crispy. Turn over and fry for a further 2–3 minutes, or until the second side is also crispy. Remove and drain on kitchen paper.

Wipe out the pan, if needed, and add 1 more tablespoon of oil. Tip in the onion and fry for a minute or two, until just softened, then add the garlic. Fry for 30 seconds or so, then add the remaining vegetables and the pineapple. Cook for a couple of minutes, then pour in the sauce. Bubble for a minute or two, until thickened, then turn off the heat.

Place the fish on serving plates and spoon over the sauce. Serve immediately, with rice.

Salmon with Tomato Sambal

Preparation time: 10 minutes

Cooking time: 20 minutes

Serves 2

—

neutral oil, for frying

1 onion, quartered and finely sliced

3 cloves of garlic, crushed

2 chillies, finely chopped (use fewer chillies or deseed if you prefer a milder heat)

2 tsp soft brown sugar

2 medium tomatoes, chopped

1 tbsp tomato purée

1½ tsp fish sauce

75ml water

2 fillets of salmon, skin on

To serve

rice

a small handful of coriander

Sambal is a chilli sauce or paste (of the spooning rather than pouring variety) with roots in many Southeast Asian countries such as Indonesia, Malaysia and Singapore. There are numerous varieties, which naturally vary from cook to cook.

The rich tomato sambal in this dish is inspired by the sweet and spicy Indonesian sambal tomat, and contrasts perfectly with the richness of the salmon.

———————

Heat 1 tablespoon of oil in a frying pan that has a lid. Fry the onion over a medium heat for a couple of minutes, then add the garlic and chillies. Fry for a further 7–10 minutes, stirring occasionally until softened.

Add the sugar, tomatoes, tomato purée, fish sauce and water, along with a good pinch of salt. Stir-fry for a minute, then reduce the heat slightly. Place the lid on and simmer for around 10 minutes, or until the tomatoes are broken down and reduced. Taste and season with salt and black pepper, if necessary.

Meanwhile, cook the salmon – you can either grill or fry it. To grill, heat the grill to high and place the salmon fillets on a greased baking sheet, skin side down. Cook under the grill for 3–5 minutes, then turn them over. Sprinkle sea salt flakes on the skin and grill for a further 3–5 minutes, until the skin is crisp and the salmon is cooked to your liking. To fry, heat 1 tablespoon of oil in a non-stick frying pan over a medium heat. Sprinkle a good pinch of sea salt flakes on the salmon skin and place it in the hot oil in the pan, skin side down. Fry for 3–4 minutes, or until the skin is golden and crisp. Turn the salmon over and cook for a further 3–4 minutes, or until cooked through.

To serve, spoon the tomato sambal on to a bowl of rice, and top with the salmon and a few coriander leaves.

Clockwise from top left: Spicy beef noodles (page 158), Spicy pineapple pickle (page 189), Crispy broccoli with spicy peanut sauce (page 26), Quick cucumber pickle (page 183), Pan-fried sea bass with spring onion, lime & chilli (page 95).

Mum's Thai Stuffed Omelette

Preparation time: 5 minutes

Cooking time: 25 minutes

Serves 2

—

For the pork filling

neutral oil, for frying

½ an onion, finely chopped

1 clove of garlic, crushed

250g pork mince, ideally over 10% fat content

2 tsp sugar

2½ tsp fish sauce

2 tsp white wine vinegar

1 tomato, diced

20g salted peanuts, chopped (optional)

For the omelette

4 eggs, beaten

To serve

rice

coriander, chopped

chilli, sliced (optional)

sweet soy sauce (kecap manis)

—

The opening recipe of my very first kitchen journal, started over twenty years ago, was this Thai stuffed omelette, known as kai yad sai. As a young child, I remember scoffing it down with relish and requesting it at every opportunity. The pork has a slight sweet-sour edge, thanks to the tomatoes and vinegar, and although it might sound like an unlikely combination, it goes great in an omelette! I personally love it with a drizzle of sweet soy sauce (kecap manis), but it's also delicious with crispy chilli oil. Usually folded into a square parcel to serve, I tend to make a normal omelette for the sake of ease.

Note: *If you can't find sweet soy sauce, simply mix 1 tablespoon of soy sauce with 1 tablespoon of honey.*

————————

Heat 1 tablespoon of oil in a frying pan over a medium heat. Add the onion and fry for 5 minutes, stirring occasionally. Add the garlic and fry for another couple of minutes, or until softened.

Add the pork mince and turn the heat up. Fry for a few minutes, until browned, making sure you break up the meat as you go. Add the sugar, fish sauce, vinegar and tomato and cook for 3–5 minutes, until the tomato starts to break down. Taste and add any extra seasoning as needed. Turn off the heat while you make the omelettes.

Heat half a tablespoon of oil in a small non-stick frying pan over a medium heat. Pour in half the eggs and swirl around the pan. Once the egg is almost cooked, place half the pork filling on one side. Sprinkle the peanuts on top of the pork, if using, then fold over. Carefully slide the omelette on to a plate and repeat.

Serve with rice, coriander, chilli and a drizzle of sweet soy sauce.

Pan-Fried Sea Bass with Spring Onion, Lime & Chilli

Preparation time: 10 minutes

Cooking time: 10–12 minutes

Serves 2

—

2 fillets of sea bass, skin on

neutral oil, for frying

2 spring onions, finely sliced

2 cloves of garlic, crushed

½–1 red chilli, finely chopped (deseed if you prefer a milder heat)

4 tsp soft brown sugar

1 tsp fish sauce

5 tbsp water

2 tbsp lime juice (approx. 1½ limes)

Delicious served with

rice

Garlicky green beans – page 168

With just 10 minutes' prep time, this is an easy dinner to throw together when you want big flavour but fancy something light. Fresh and citrusy with a bit of sweet heat, the quick pan sauce pairs deliciously with the sea bass, but would also work well with salmon.

Note: *This dish cooks quickly, so make sure you have all the ingredients prepped and near the stove before you start cooking.*

———————

Dry the sea bass skin with kitchen paper and sprinkle with sea salt. Heat 1 tablespoon of oil in a large non-stick frying pan over a medium-high heat. Once very hot, carefully place the sea bass in the pan, skin side down. Press down on each fillet to make sure the skin has full contact with the pan.

Fry untouched for 2½–3 minutes, or until the skin is golden and crispy, then flip over. Reduce the heat to medium-low and cook for a further 2 more minutes, or until cooked. Remove from the pan and place on a plate, skin side up.

Heat another tablespoon of oil over a medium heat. Add the spring onions, garlic and red chilli and cook for 1 minute, until softened. Add the sugar, fish sauce and water and turn up the heat. Bubble for 1–2 minutes, until around half of the liquid has evaporated. Add the lime juice and bubble for a further minute or so, then remove from the heat.

Pour over the sea bass and eat immediately.

Hong Kong-Style Rice Pot

**Preparation time: 20 minutes
+ 10 minutes resting time**

Cooking time: 25 minutes

Serves 4 generously

—

For the pork

3 tbsp light soy sauce

2 tbsp oyster sauce

½ tbsp caster sugar

2 tsp sesame oil,
    preferably toasted

3 cloves of garlic, crushed

1 tbsp grated ginger
    (approx. 6cm)

1 pork fillet, approx. 450g,
    sliced ½cm thick

For the rice

150g mushrooms, sliced

4 spring onions, cut into
    5cm pieces

2–3 pak choi (depending on size),
    quartered lengthways

300g jasmine rice

350ml chicken stock

A twist on the usual fried rice, I first heard about this one-pot dish through my half-Chinese friend Melissa Ng and her dad, who shared their recipe with me, which inspired this version. Traditionally made in a clay pot, and often with chicken, the meat and veg steam while the rice cooks. The marinade seeps into the rice, adding moisture and inbuilt seasoning. Leftovers are delicious with a fried egg.

Note: *Don't be alarmed if the bottom of the rice becomes a bit burnt – this is part of the dish and adds a lovely charred flavour.*

———————————

Mix the soy sauce, oyster sauce, sugar, sesame oil, garlic and ginger together in a dish. Add the pork and coat well. Leave to marinate for at least 10 minutes.

Now's a good time to prep the mushrooms, spring onions and pak choi, if you haven't already. Rinse the rice in a sieve.

Place the rice and stock in a large saucepan or stoneware pot and give it a little stir. Put the lid on and bring to the boil. Place the mushrooms and spring onions on top in an even layer. Replace the lid and cook on a medium-low heat for 10 minutes, then add the pork, along with its marinade, in an even layer. Replace the lid and cook for 5 minutes, before adding an even layer of pak choi. Replace the lid again and cook for a final 5 minutes.

Turn off the heat and leave to rest for 10 minutes. The rice and pork should be cooked through and the pak choi just cooked. If not, replace the lid for another few minutes.

Before serving, give the dish a gentle mix, scraping the bottom while it's warm. Feel free to drizzle with any extra soy, sweet soy or crispy chilli oil at the table.

Hot & Zingy Prawn Broth

Preparation time: 5 minutes

Cooking time: 5 minutes

Serves 2 as a starter or light lunch

—

600ml chicken stock

2cm ginger, sliced

1 red bird's-eye chilli, finely chopped

150g raw peeled prawns

2 tsp fish sauce

2–4 tsp lime juice (approx. ½–1 lime)

a pinch of caster sugar (optional)

To serve

a small handful of coriander, chopped

David Thompson's epic *Thai Food* bible has sat proudly on my bookshelf for the last twenty years, and it was his recipe for 'prawn soup with slices of lime' that provided the inspiration for this dish. I have taken some liberties and edged it very slightly towards tom yum territory, with the addition of chillies and fish sauce, but the concept of simplicity remains. A great little starter as part of a bigger Asian-inspired feast, but you could add some cooked thin noodles to your bowl, or a few sliced mushrooms (at the ginger stage), to turn it into a light lunch.

Note: *If you can't find bird's-eye chillies or you find them too hot, substitute regular red chillies. Similarly, if you can take the heat, feel free to add more!*

Note: *The sliced ginger is there to infuse its flavour rather than to be eaten. If, however, you would prefer to eat it, I suggest cutting it into matchsticks instead.*

Put the chicken stock into a medium-sized pan with the ginger and bring to the boil. Add the chilli and prawns and cook until the prawns are just done.

Turn off the heat and add the fish sauce and 2 teaspoons of lime juice. The broth should be hot, sour and salty. Taste and add extra lime juice, fish sauce or sugar, as needed.

Top with coriander and serve.

Spicy Shakshuka

Preparation time: 5 minutes

Cooking time: 30 minutes

Serves 2

—

neutral oil, for frying

1 onion, thinly sliced

2 cloves of garlic, crushed

1 red pepper, thinly sliced

1 x 400g tin of chopped tomatoes

1 tbsp chilli bean paste (see note, page 12)

½–1 tsp caster sugar (according to taste)

4 eggs

To serve

a handful of coriander, chopped

crusty bread, rice or Roti – page 174

Shakshuka is a great storecupboard dish to have up your sleeve. Easy to make, healthy and of course delicious – what's not to love? In this recipe I've given the flavours an Asian-style twist with a spoonful of chilli bean paste (see page 12) for a back note of warm umami heat.

———————

Heat 1 tablespoon of oil in a large frying pan that has a lid over a medium heat. Add the onion and garlic and fry for 5 minutes, stirring occasionally until soft. Add the red pepper and cook for a further 2–3 minutes.

Add the tinned tomatoes, chilli bean paste, and ½ a teaspoon of sugar, along with half a tin of water, and bring to a simmer. Lower the heat and bubble for around 10 minutes, until thickened and reduced slightly, stirring occasionally. Taste, and if you would like some extra heat, add an extra teaspoon of chilli bean paste (be warned – it is exceptionally salty, so add gradually!). Check for seasoning and add any extra salt or sugar, if needed.

Make 4 wells in the sauce and crack an egg into each one. Place the lid on top (or a piece of tight-fitting foil) and simmer on a medium heat for 3–4 minutes, or until the eggs are cooked to your liking.

Serve with freshly chopped coriander and crusty bread, rice or Roti.

Curries

Thai Red Beef & Peanut Curry

Preparation time: 10 minutes

Cooking time: 10 minutes

Serves 4

—

1 tbsp neutral oil, for frying

2 tbsp Thai red curry paste

450g sirloin or rump steak, thinly sliced

1 x 400ml tin of coconut milk

2 tbsp unsweetened crunchy peanut butter

1–2 tsp fish sauce (to taste)

1–1½ tbsp soft brown sugar (to taste)

100g green beans, cut in half diagonally

40g salted peanuts, roughly chopped (optional)

red chilli, finely sliced (optional)

Delicious served with

rice

Roti – page 174

Cucumber relish – page 183

The aroma of Thai red curry paste sizzling in hot oil instantly throws me back to childhood. My mother frequently had a pot of curry on the go, usually made with beef, and always served with steamed rice.

However, although Thai curries are a weekly staple, I have a confession to make: I never make my own paste. The truth is, time is short, and there are some fantastic ones available to buy out there. My Thai friends reassure me this is what the busy Bangkokians do, and if it's good enough for them, then I'm happy!

Here I have added peanut butter, taking the curry somewhere towards a mellow massaman via my old friend satay. The fact that it takes less than half an hour to cook makes it all the more delicious.

Note: *I use 2 tablespoons of Mae Ploy Thai red curry paste (which is spicier than many others), but if you prefer it on the mild side, then add less. Curry pastes do vary in heat, so taste and tweak as necessary.*

———

Heat the oil in a large frying pan or wok over a high heat. Stir-fry the curry paste for a few moments until it becomes fragrant. Add the beef and stir-fry for another minute or so, making sure all the strips are coated in the paste.

Lower the heat to medium, then add the coconut milk, peanut butter, 1 teaspoon of fish sauce and 1 tablespoon of sugar. Stir to combine and taste to assess the heat level and depth of flavour from the paste. If you need more, add it here (loosen with water first, if needed), then simmer for a minute. Add the green beans and simmer for another couple of minutes, or until the beans are just cooked. Taste the sauce, and add a pinch of salt, and any extra fish sauce or sugar, if needed.

Before serving, scatter over the chopped peanuts and red chilli, if using.

Sweet Potato & Black Bean Traybake Curry

Preparation time: 20 minutes

Cooking time: 45–50 minutes

Serves 4

—

1 stalk of lemongrass

1 onion, finely chopped

3 cloves of garlic, crushed

1 tbsp grated ginger (approx. 6cm)

700g sweet potatoes, skin on, cut into approx. 2–3cm pieces

3 tbsp curry powder (whichever heat preferred)

1 tsp ground cinnamon

1 x 400ml tin of coconut milk

400ml veg or chicken stock, or water

300g cherry tomatoes

1 x 400g tin of black beans, drained

75g green beans, halved

To serve

rice

Although I'm happy to stand over a hot stove, there are times when I'd rather let the oven do all the work. Ideal for when you've got guests over and would prefer to chat rather than cook (definitely my inclination if given the choice!), or when you need a tasty dinner that looks after itself while you negotiate the children's bedtime.

———————————

Preheat the oven to 200°C/180°C fan/gas mark 6.

Prepare the lemongrass. Remove the tough outer leaves and trim off the top end. Bash it with the end of a rolling pin, then chop it as finely as possible.

Place the lemongrass, onion, garlic and ginger in a large oven dish or tray. Add the sweet potatoes, then sprinkle over the curry powder, cinnamon and 1 teaspoon of salt. Pour in the coconut milk, then the stock or water, and stir until mixed (don't worry if the coconut milk is lumpy at this point, it will dissolve as it cooks). The dish will look quite liquidy at this stage but it will reduce and thicken once it cooks. Add the cherry tomatoes, then place in the oven for 30 minutes.

Take the dish out of the oven and add the black and green beans. Cook for a further 15–20 minutes or so, until the sweet potato is soft. Taste for seasoning and add salt and pepper as needed. Serve with rice.

Thai Yellow Chicken Curry

Preparation time: 15 minutes

Cooking time: 30 minutes

Serves 2

—

1 stalk of lemongrass

neutral oil, for frying

½ an onion, finely chopped

2 cloves of garlic, crushed

1 tsp grated ginger (approx. 2cm)

2 red chillies, finely chopped

1 tsp curry powder (whichever heat preferred)

½ tsp ground turmeric

200ml coconut milk

200ml chicken or veg stock, or water

1 tsp fish sauce

1 chicken breast, finely sliced

½ a red pepper, cut into thin strips

a pinch of caster sugar (optional)

To serve

rice

Hailing from southern Thailand, yellow curry may not be as familiar as its red or green cousins but its rich tones more than hold its own. Aromatic, creamy and subtly spiced, this gorgeous curry can be made in around 45 minutes and is one you'll keep coming back to.

———————

Prepare the lemongrass. Remove the tough outer leaves and bash with a rolling pin, then cut in half.

Heat 1 tablespoon of oil in a large frying pan or wok over a medium heat. Add the onion, garlic, ginger, lemongrass and chillies and cook for 5–7 minutes, until softened, stirring occasionally. Add the curry powder and turmeric and stir-fry for a further minute.

Add the coconut milk and the water or stock, along with the fish sauce, and simmer for 10 minutes, stirring occasionally.

Add the chicken and cook for 2–3 minutes, stirring occasionally, then tip in the peppers. Simmer for a few more minutes, again stirring occasionally, until the chicken and peppers are cooked. Remove the lemongrass stalk, taste the sauce for seasoning and add any extra fish sauce or salt, and a pinch of sugar, if necessary. Serve with rice.

Spinach & Turmeric Fish Curry

Preparation time: 15 minutes

Cooking time: 30 minutes

Serves 4

—

neutral oil, for frying

1 onion, finely chopped

2 cloves of garlic, crushed

2 tbsp grated ginger (approx. 10–12cm)

2 red chillies, finely chopped

1 tsp ground turmeric

1 x 400ml tin of coconut milk

2 tsp light soy sauce

¼ tsp salt

200g spinach

4 skinless white fish fillets (approx. 500g), e.g. hake or cod, cut into large chunks (approx. 6cm)

To serve

red chillies, finely sliced

A gentle, understated but entirely delicious curry. My kids absolutely love it (without the chilli), and I've even caught them licking the cold pan in the kitchen after tea to get every last bit of sauce. If that's not a successful dish, I don't know what is.

Note: *Omit the chilli for a child-friendly version, and feel free to add a few prawns as well as or instead of the fish.*

———————————

Heat 1 tablespoon of oil in a large frying pan that has a lid over a medium heat. Fry the onion, garlic, ginger and chillies for 5–7 minutes, stirring occasionally, until softened. Add the turmeric and fry for a further 2 minutes or so, making sure it doesn't burn.

Add the coconut milk, soy sauce and salt and bring to a simmer. Cook for 5 minutes or so, stirring occasionally. Taste the sauce and add any extra seasoning, if necessary.

Add the spinach to the pan, stirring to coat it in the sauce, then nestle the fish on top. Put the lid on, reduce to medium-low and cook for 5–10 minutes, or until the spinach has wilted and the fish is cooked through. Serve immediately, sprinkled with extra red chillies, if desired.

Dry Beef & Coconut Curry

Preparation time: 10 minutes

Cooking time: 40 minutes

Serves 4

—

2 stalks of lemongrass

neutral oil, for frying

1 tsp ground turmeric

1 tbsp grated ginger (approx. 6cm)

2 cloves of garlic, crushed

1 tsp dried red chilli flakes

1 tsp ground coriander

50g desiccated coconut, toasted

1 x 400ml tin of coconut milk

½ tsp salt

1½ tsp caster sugar

500g sirloin steak, trimmed of
  excess fat, thinly sliced

Delicious served with

rice

Spicy pineapple pickle – page 189

A departure from the usual saucy variety, this Indonesian-inspired dry curry uses coconut milk and desiccated coconut as the base. Along with lemongrass, ginger and spices, the coconut is reduced down until the 'sauce' becomes paste-like. The result is a rich, mellow, aromatic dish, delicious as part of a bigger feast or on its own with rice, my Garlicky green beans (page 168) and Malaysian-style pickled vegetables (page 184) or Spicy pineapple pickle (page 189).

Note: *Some coconut milks release more oil than others, so serve the curry with a slotted spoon to leave some of that oil behind, if you prefer.*

———————

Prepare the lemongrass. Remove the tough outer leaves and bash with a rolling pin, then cut in half.

Place 1 tablespoon of oil in a large frying pan over a low-medium heat and add the turmeric, ginger, garlic, chilli flakes and coriander. Fry for 2 minutes, stirring constantly, making sure it doesn't burn.

Add the desiccated coconut, coconut milk, lemongrass, salt and sugar. Turn up the heat and bring to the boil, stirring occasionally. Reduce the heat to low and simmer for around 25 minutes, again stirring occasionally.

As the curry cooks the coconut will start releasing oil – don't be alarmed. The curry will also change in colour from pale yellow to golden, and the liquid will have reduced and become paste-like. Once this has happened, turn the heat back to medium-high and add the steak. Stir-fry for a few minutes until just cooked, making sure the meat is completely coated in the coconut. Remove the lemongrass stalk, taste the curry for seasoning, adding extra salt or sugar, as necessary, and serve the curry with rice.

Chinese-Style Pea & Aubergine Curry

Preparation time: 5 minutes

Cooking time: 25 minutes

Serves 2

—

neutral oil, for frying

1 medium aubergine, cut into
approximately 3cm cubes

1 tsp cornflour

300ml veg or chicken stock

½ an onion, sliced

1½ tsp curry powder (whichever
heat preferred)

½ tsp ground turmeric

¼ tsp chilli powder

½ tsp caster sugar

50g frozen peas

To serve

rice

It's amazing how a handful of simple ingredients can come together to produce something so luscious. This modest curry is made with readily available storecupboard spices, yet has a luxurious feel thanks to the rich, soft aubergines. The burst of sweetness from the peas brightens up each mouthful and the moreish sauce will have you coming back for more.

Note: *You could use tofu or thinly sliced chicken breast in place of the aubergine. If using chicken, you will need to fry it for a shorter time at the beginning and won't need to bubble it for as long in the sauce – just until it is cooked.*

———————

Heat 2 tablespoons of oil in a large frying pan over a medium heat. Add the aubergine along with a good pinch or two of salt. Fry for 7–10 minutes, until browned all over and tender, turning frequently.

Meanwhile, mix the cornflour with 1 tablespoon of the stock and set near the stove.

Remove the aubergines from the pan. Add another tablespoon of oil to the pan, then add the onions and fry for a couple of minutes. Add the curry powder, turmeric, chilli powder and sugar and cook for a further 2 minutes.

Add the rest of the stock along with the cornflour mix, then put back the aubergine. Bubble gently for 5–10 minutes, until the aubergines are soft and cooked through, stirring occasionally and adding a splash of water if it gets too thick. Tip in the peas and heat for a minute or two, until cooked. Serve with rice.

Fiery Cauliflower, Chickpea & Spinach Curry

Preparation time: 5 minutes

Cooking time: 15–20 minutes

Serves 4

—

neutral oil, for frying

2 tbsp Thai red curry paste

1 tsp ground turmeric

600ml veg stock

½–1 tsp soft brown sugar

1 cauliflower, cut into small bite-
  sized florets

1 x 400g tin of chickpeas, drained

100g spinach

To serve

rice

red chillies, finely sliced (optional)

On days when you crave a spicy curry, but want clean and bright flavours, this one's for you. Inspired by the broth-like fiery Thai jungle curry, this is a delicious fresh alternative to the usual coconut-based variety. While this version may not be nearly as hot as the original jungle curry, it still has a good tongue-tingling amount of heat, especially if you're using Mae Ploy curry paste, like I do. Feel free to add more chillies if you can take it! Likewise, use less paste to begin with if you're unsure about the spice level – you can always add more as you go.

———————

Heat 1 tablespoon of oil in a large saucepan or lidded wok over a low-medium heat. Fry the curry paste and turmeric, stirring constantly for a minute or so, until the paste starts to change colour and releases its aroma.

Add the stock to the pan with half a teaspoon of sugar, then have a taste – curry pastes can vary, so if you're not getting enough flavour, add a little more paste now. Stir in the cauliflower and chickpeas. Cover, turn the heat up and bring to the boil, then lower the heat slightly. Simmer for 5 minutes, then stir in the spinach. Cook for another few minutes, until the cauliflower is tender and the spinach is wilted. Taste the curry for seasoning and add any extra sugar, salt or pepper, as needed. Serve with rice, and extra chillies, if desired.

Stir-Fries

Singapore-Style Chilli Tofu

Preparation time: 20 minutes

Cooking time: 30 minutes

Serves 2

—

40g cashew nuts

neutral oil, for frying

200g firm tofu, dried with kitchen paper and cut into bite-sized cubes

1 onion, finely chopped

1 tbsp grated ginger (approx. 3cm)

3 cloves of garlic, crushed

2 red chillies, finely chopped (use fewer chillies or deseed if you prefer a milder heat)

1 medium tomato, diced

200ml hot veg or chicken stock, or boiling water

½ a medium head of broccoli or 150g tenderstem broccoli, cut into small florets

1 small egg, lightly beaten

For the sauce

4 tbsp tomato ketchup

2 tbsp sweet chilli sauce

1 tbsp light soy sauce

1 tsp sesame oil, preferably toasted

To serve

rice

This recipe was inspired by the stunning dish Singapore-style chilli prawns, which is itself a version of the famous Singapore chilli crab. Tofu can sometimes get a bad rap, but it makes a fantastic alternative to prawns, especially midweek. It has a relatively long shelf-life, so is great to have on hand in the fridge. Frying it until crispy gives it great texture, and it absorbs all the flavours of the sauce – and this dish is ALL about the sauce. It even converted my tofu-fearing husband.

Note: *The egg thickens the sauce, and adds a lovely richness and flavour, but can easily be omitted for a vegan version.*

———————————

Toast the cashews in a large non-stick frying pan over a medium heat until golden. Remove from the pan and set aside.

Add 1 tablespoon of oil to the pan and when hot, add the tofu and fry for 5–10 minutes, until all sides are golden. Remove from the pan and set aside.

Meanwhile, mix the sauce ingredients together in a small bowl and place near the stove.

Wipe any excess tofu crumbs from the pan, then add another tablespoon of oil. Reduce the heat to medium-low and add the onions, ginger, garlic and chillies along with a pinch of salt. Cook for 7–10 minutes, stirring occasionally, until softened. Add another drizzle of oil, if necessary.

Add the tomatoes along with the sauce and simmer for 3–5 minutes, or until the tomatoes have reduced down. Stir frequently to prevent it sticking to the pan, adding a splash of water, if needed.

Pour in the hot stock or water, turn the heat to medium and bring to a simmer. Add the broccoli and coat in the sauce. Cook for a couple of minutes, then pour in the egg, and stir to mix. Return the tofu to the pan and cook for a further minute, until heated through and the broccoli is just cooked. Loosen the sauce with a little water, if needed, then taste for seasoning and adjust as necessary.

Just before serving, stir through the toasted cashews. Serve with rice.

Hoisin Shiitake Mushrooms

Preparation time: 10 minutes

Cooking time: 10 minutes

Serves 2 as a light meal

—

For the stir-fry

250g shiitake mushrooms, cut into thick slices (smaller ones halved or kept whole)

2 tbsp cornflour

3 spring onions, cut into 5cm pieces

1½ tbsp hoisin sauce

3 tbsp neutral oil, for frying

For the sauce

1 tbsp light soy sauce

1 tsp Chinese 5-spice

2 tsp sesame oil, preferably toasted

3 cloves of garlic, crushed

1 tsp honey

1 tsp dried red chilli flakes (optional)

6 tbsp water

To serve

spring onion, finely sliced

rice

Bottles and jars of every type of sauce and condiment fill my storecupboard shelves – I'm hopelessly addicted and can't stop adding to my collection. If I had to choose a top five (a pretty hard task), hoisin would undoubtedly make the cut. I've been hooked ever since my first mouthful of crispy duck pancake as a child and I now use it frequently as a cooking ingredient in stir-fries and noodle dishes.

Here, the wonderful meaty texture of the shiitake mushrooms is a perfect match for the barbecued sweetness of the hoisin. Super quick and wickedly delicious, this is a brilliant recipe to have up your sleeve.

Note: *If you can't get hold of shiitake mushrooms, then the chestnut variety make a great substitute.*

———————————

Place the mushrooms in a mixing bowl and sprinkle over the cornflour. Toss well.

Make the sauce. In a small bowl combine all the ingredients.

Heat the oil in a large non-stick frying pan or wok over a medium-high heat, and when very hot add the mushrooms, shaking off any excess flour. Fry for 5 minutes, stirring occasionally. Add the spring onion pieces and cook for a further 2–3 minutes.

Once the mushrooms have taken on some colour, reduce the heat to low and stir in the sauce, making sure the mushrooms are well coated. Simmer for a minute or two, then remove from the heat and serve immediately, with the sliced spring onions and rice.

Stir-Fried Pork with Basil

Preparation time: 10 minutes

Cooking time: 15 minutes

Serves 2

—

1 tbsp oyster sauce

½ tbsp light soy sauce

2 tsp caster sugar

2 tbsp water

neutral oil, for frying

½ an onion, finely chopped

2 cloves of garlic, crushed

1–2 bird's-eye or red chillies (depending on heat preference), finely chopped

250g pork mince, ideally over 10% fat content

50g green beans, halved

a large handful of basil leaves

To serve

2 eggs

rice

chilli oil or sweet soy sauce

Based on another Thai classic, pad kra pao (holy basil stir-fry), this particular recipe actually started life as a simple pork stir-fry for the kids, with no chillies or basil, as a way of introducing them to Thai flavours. They loved it. Of course, being a chilli addict, I couldn't resist putting back a couple, along with the basil, which adds a wonderful aromatic layer of flavour. I use standard Italian basil, which is widely available and works perfectly, but if you are able to get hold of holy basil then all the better. While this recipe may not be as fiery as the usual pad kra pao, it still has a good amount of heat and makes a heavenly plate of food. Feel free to add three or four more garlic cloves and extra chillies, if you're up for it!

Note: *If you use lower-fat mince then you may need to add a splash of water at the end, if it seems a little dry.*

———————

Combine the oyster sauce, soy sauce, sugar and water in a small bowl and place near the stove.

Heat 1 tablespoon of oil in a large frying pan or wok over a medium heat. Add the onion and stir-fry for 3–4 minutes, until starting to soften. Add the garlic and chillies and cook for a further minute or two.

Turn the heat up to medium-high and add the pork mince. You may need to drizzle in some extra oil. Cook for a few minutes, until browned, making sure you break up the meat as you go.

Stir in the green beans, then add the sauce and stir-fry for a minute or two. Once the beans are cooked, stir through the basil. Turn off the heat, taste and add an extra splash of soy, if necessary.

In a separate pan, heat a drizzle of oil and fry the eggs until cooked to your liking.

Serve the pork with rice, topped with a fried egg. Delicious with a drizzle of chilli oil or sweet soy sauce.

Tomato & Chilli Halloumi

Preparation time: 10 minutes

Cooking time: 20 minutes

Serves 2

—

For the sauce

1 tbsp tomato purée

1 tbsp rice vinegar

1 tbsp sriracha

1 tbsp light soy sauce

1 tbsp honey

5 tbsp water

For the stir-fry

neutral oil, for frying

1 x 250g block of halloumi, cut
     into bite-sized cubes

1 onion, finely sliced

4 cloves of garlic, crushed

1 red chilli, finely chopped

1 red pepper, sliced

2 tomatoes, chopped

To serve

coriander leaves (optional)

rice

Delicious served with

Garlicky green beans – page 168

Oh, how I love halloumi. I can't resist its gorgeous chewy saltiness and always have a block or two in the fridge. Usually I have it just as it comes, sizzling from the pan, or cut into squares and added to soups for a salty hit.

Here, however, it's the star of a stunning, spicy, tomato-rich stir-fry. If you're a halloumi fan like me, this will be on your repeat list!

———————

Make the sauce. Combine all the ingredients and set aside.

Heat a drizzle of oil in a large non-stick frying pan or wok over a medium heat. Add the halloumi and fry for around 4–5 minutes, turning occasionally, until golden all over. Remove and wipe out the pan, if necessary.

Heat another 1 tablespoon of oil and fry the onion, garlic and chilli for 5 minutes, stirring occasionally until softened. Add the red pepper and tomatoes and stir-fry for 2–3 minutes. Pour in the sauce, then turn down the heat slightly and gently bubble for 2 minutes.

Put the halloumi back into the pan and coat with the sauce. Cook for another couple of minutes to warm through, loosening with a splash of water, if needed. Serve immediately topped with coriander, if using, and rice.

Fridge-Raid Stir-Fried Rice

Preparation time: 10 minutes

Cooking time: 10 minutes

Serves 2

—

neutral oil, for frying

½ an onion or leek or a few spring onions, thinly sliced

2 cloves of garlic, crushed

200–250g vegetables, sliced, diced or cut into small florets

250g cooked rice (about 110g uncooked weight of jasmine rice or 90g of basmati)

1 egg

1 tbsp light soy sauce

1 tbsp oyster sauce

To serve

spring onions, finely sliced (optional)

coriander leaves (optional)

chilli oil (optional)

If your fridge is anything like mine, then a good fridge-raid is a bit of a necessity every now and then – and what better way to cook all those odds and ends than with this stir-fried rice dish. This recipe is all about flexibility – use up what you have and feel free to add leftover prawns or any meat you might have as well. I tend to go for crunchy veg like broccoli, red pepper, carrot and sugar snap peas.

Cold day-old rice is ideal, but you can also make some fresh and spread it out on a plate to cool.

———————

Heat 1 tablespoon of oil in a large non-stick frying pan or wok over a medium-high heat. Add the onion or leek and stir-fry for a couple of minutes, until starting to soften, then add the garlic and fry for a further minute. If using spring onions, fry with the garlic for just 1 minute or so.

Add the veg and stir-fry for another few minutes, until almost cooked, then tip in the rice and combine. Push to one side, then crack in the egg (you may need to add a drizzle of oil if the pan is a bit dry). Scramble until set, then stir it through the rice.

Add the soy sauce and oyster sauce and combine well. Stir-fry for another minute or so, until everything is coated in the sauce and the rice is hot. Serve immediately.

Lemongrass & Tamarind Stir-Fried Tofu

Preparation time: 10 minutes

Cooking time: 15 minutes

Serves 2

—

1 stalk of lemongrass

3 tbsp soft brown sugar

2 tbsp tamarind paste
  (see note, page 15)

2 tbsp light soy sauce

2 tbsp water

neutral oil, for frying

200g extra firm tofu, dried with
  kitchen paper and cut into bite-
  sized cubes

1 onion, finely sliced

2 cloves of garlic, crushed

1 tsp grated ginger (approx. 2cm)

1 red chilli, finely chopped

To serve

rice

If you love stir-fries but find yourself stuck for inspiration, look no further! Loosely based on the Indonesian dish tempeh sambal goreng, which uses tempeh as the main ingredient, this recipe heroes tofu and is an explosion of flavour – spicy, sticky, sour, sweet and aromatic all at once.

Prawns, chicken or pork fillet would work equally well in place of the tofu, as would aubergines.

———————

Prepare the lemongrass. Remove the tough outer leaves and bash with a rolling pin, then cut in half. Set aside. Combine the sugar, tamarind paste, soy sauce and water, and place near the stove.

Heat 1 tablespoon of oil in a large non-stick frying pan over a medium-high heat. Add the tofu and fry for 5–10 minutes, or until golden on all sides. Remove and wipe away any excess crumbs from the pan.

Lower the heat to medium, add another tablespoon of oil and fry the onion, garlic, ginger, chilli and lemongrass for 5 minutes, stirring occasionally until soft. Add the sauce, let it bubble for a moment, then put the tofu back into the pan and stir to coat. Stir-fry for another minute or two. Remove the lemongrass stalk before serving.

Serve with rice. Also delicious with broccoli.

Stir-Fried Rice
with Gochujang Beef

Preparation time: 15 minutes

Cooking time: 10 minutes

Serves 2

—

For the sauce

2 tbsp gochujang paste

2½ tbsp light soy sauce

1 tsp honey

For the rice

200–250g rump or sirloin steak, trimmed of excess fat and sinew, thinly sliced

3 spring onions

2 cloves of garlic

1 carrot

½ a courgette

neutral oil, for frying

250g cooked rice (approx. 110g uncooked weight of jasmine rice, 90g if using basmati)

To serve

2 eggs

1 spring onion, finely sliced (optional)

Since having kids, going out for dinner outside my postcode is a rare luxury (in fact, going to the supermarket alone is a rare luxury these days!). Inspired by fond memories of bibimbap in many a Korean restaurant over the years, I came up with this stir-fry to satisfy my craving. A tasty plate of food you can have ready in under half an hour. Sounds good to me.

———————————

Combine the ingredients for the sauce in a small bowl.

Place the steak in a separate bowl and add 1 tablespoon of the sauce. Stir to coat, then set aside to marinate while you prepare the rest of the dish.

Finely slice the spring onions and crush the garlic. Cut the carrot and courgette into thin batons.

Heat 1 tablespoon of oil in a large non-stick frying pan or wok over a medium heat. Add the spring onions and garlic and cook for a minute or so. Turn up the heat to high and add the marinated beef. Stir-fry for 1 minute, until seared all over, then add the carrot and courgette and stir-fry for a further minute.

Add the rice and combine, then add the remaining sauce, reserving 1 tablespoon for drizzling at the table.

Stir-fry for a couple of minutes, until the rice is completely coated and hot through. Take off the heat.

In a separate frying pan, heat a drizzle of oil and fry the eggs until done to your liking. Divide the rice between two dishes and top with the eggs and spring onion, if using. Serve the reserved sauce at the table for optional drizzling.

Thai Red Curry
Chicken Stir-Fry

Preparation time: 10 minutes

Cooking time: 10 minutes

Serves 2

—

For the sauce

1 tbsp oyster sauce

1 tbsp sweet chilli sauce

½ tsp fish sauce

1 tsp caster sugar

150ml water

For the stir-fry

neutral oil, for frying

2 tbsp Thai red curry paste

1 chicken breast, thinly sliced

½ a red pepper, sliced

75g green beans, halved on
    the diagonal

a handful of basil leaves

To serve

rice

Whether it was my mum or my aunt who first showed me how to make this, I can't recall. What I do know is that when I want a quick dinner fix, full of chilli-tingling goodness, this fiery stir-fry is what I turn to. A take on the Thai dish prik king, this is a gutsy alternative to the usual red curry.

Note: *This dish would work equally well with tofu, prawns, beef or pork fillet (if using tofu, fry separately until golden and crisp, then add to the pan in place of the chicken). I use May Ploy Thai red curry paste (which is spicier than many others), but if you prefer it on the mild side, then add less.*

In a small bowl combine the sauce ingredients. Place near the stove.

Heat 1 tablespoon of oil in a large frying pan or wok over a medium-high heat. Add the curry paste and cook for 30 seconds, stirring constantly. Add the chicken and stir-fry for 2 minutes.

Add the red pepper and green beans and stir-fry for 1 minute, then pour in the sauce and stir-fry for 1–2 minutes, until just cooked but still with some bite and the chicken is cooked through. Taste the sauce – if it's not spicy enough, stir in a little more curry paste (loosen with water first, if needed). Add an extra pinch of sugar or a few more drops of fish sauce, if necessary.

Finally, stir through the basil leaves until wilted, then turn off the heat. Serve with rice.

Kung Pao-Style Brussels Sprouts with Chorizo

Preparation time: 15 minutes

Cooking time: 15 minutes

Serves 2 as a main

—

8 large dried whole red chillies

2 raw chorizo sausages

50g cashew nuts

2 tbsp neutral oil, for frying

400g Brussels sprouts, ends trimmed and outer leaves removed, halved

1 tsp grated ginger (approx. 2cm)

3 cloves of garlic, sliced

1 tsp Sichuan peppercorns, ground

For the sauce

1 tsp cornflour

3 tbsp water

1 tbsp light soy sauce

2 tbsp caster sugar

2 tbsp rice vinegar

To serve

rice

Brussels sprouts may be synonymous with Christmas, but they are actually in season in the UK from October through to March. These mini cabbages are so much more than just a festive side dish, and here they are given their opportunity to shine. Charring them brings out their best, and when you add a spicy, sweet sauce, along with slices of smoky, salty chorizo, you have something quite spectacular. Brussels sprout haters, beware – this might just convert you.

Note: *This dish cooks quickly, so make sure you have all the elements prepared before you start.*

———————

In a bowl, mix the cornflour with 1 tablespoon of water, then combine with the soy, sugar, rice vinegar and remaining 2 tablespoons of water. Set aside.

Snip the stalks off the chillies with scissors and empty out the seeds. Cut into roughly 3cm pieces.

Cut each chorizo lengthways, then slice to give half-moons.

Heat a large frying pan or wok over a medium heat and toast the cashews until golden, then remove and set aside.

Add a drizzle of oil to the pan and fry the chorizo for a minute or two, until cooked. Remove with a slotted spoon and set aside.

Add the Brussels sprouts to the chorizo oil and turn up the heat to medium-high. Add a drizzle more oil if necessary. Fry for a few minutes until nicely charred, stirring occasionally. Remove and set aside.

Turn the heat down to medium, then add 2 tablespoons of oil. Once hot, add the ginger, garlic and Sichuan peppercorns and stir-fry for a few moments, until aromatic. Add the dried chillies and stir-fry for another 30 seconds or so, being sure not to burn the chillies. Turn down the heat slightly, then pour in the sauce, stirring to make sure it doesn't burn. Bubble for a few moments and once the sauce has thickened, return the sprouts to the pan along with the chorizo. Make sure everything is nicely coated before stirring in the cashews. Serve immediately, with rice.

Noodles

Sesame Ramen
with Caramelized Pork

Preparation time: 25 minutes

Cooking time: 25 minutes

Serves 2 generously

—

For the paste

6 tbsp tahini

1 tbsp Thai red curry paste

2½ tbsp soft brown sugar

2 tbsp light soy sauce

1 tbsp grated ginger (approx. 6cm)

For the pork

2 spring onions, finely sliced

1 tsp grated ginger (approx. 2cm)

1 clove of garlic, crushed

1 red chilli, finely sliced

200g pork mince, preferably
    15–20% fat content

2½ tbsp honey

1½ tbsp fish sauce

For the noodles

2 large eggs

800ml chicken stock

100g tenderstem broccoli,
    cut into 5cm pieces

2 portions of ramen or medium
    egg or wheat noodles

1 carrot, shredded with a julienne
    peeler or cut into matchsticks

1 spring onion, finely sliced

Being half Thai I eat more than my fair share of noodles – there's nothing better than a bowl of warming ramen to lift the spirits and fly you off to a different continent. This recipe uses Thai red curry paste and tahini to create a spicy, rich, nutty broth. It might sound strange, but I promise it works! Sweet and savoury caramelized pork takes this dish to a whole other level.

Note: *While this recipe has a number of elements, none of them are complicated, and the end result is undoubtedly worth the effort! You can substitute the pork with prawns, leftover chicken or more veg, if you wish.*

———————

Whisk the paste ingredients together and divide between two serving bowls. Cook the noodles according to instructions then rinse well under cold water. Set aside.

Heat a large frying pan over a medium heat and add 1 tablespoon of oil. Add the spring onions, ginger, garlic and chilli, and stir-fry for 1 minute. Add the pork, turn up to medium-high and fry for 4–5 minutes, breaking up the meat as you go, until browned and starting to dry out. Mix in the honey and fish sauce and stir-fry for a further couple of minutes. Turn off the heat. Set aside.

Fill a small saucepan with boiling water and bring to the boil over a medium heat. Add the eggs and cook for 6 minutes, then immediately remove and run under cold water for a minute or so. Peel and cut in half.

Bring the stock to the boil in a large pan. Add the broccoli and cook for 2–3 minutes, until just done. Remove and set aside. Add the cooked noodles and turn down the heat – you want them to reheat, not cook. Add a ladle of stock to each serving bowl and whisk to combine, then stir in the remaining stock.

Add the noodles, and top with the caramelized pork, the halved soft-boiled eggs, the broccoli and shredded carrot. Garnish with spring onions. Nice with a drizzle of soy or chilli oil.

Auntie Dang's Stir-Fried Soy Sauce Noodles

Preparation time: 15 minutes

Cooking time: 10 minutes

Serves 2 generously

—

200g dried wide rice noodles

3 tbsp light soy sauce

3 tbsp oyster sauce

1 tbsp caster sugar

neutral oil, for frying

1 x 200g sirloin or rump steak, very thinly sliced

2 cloves of garlic, crushed

1 carrot, cut into thin batons

100g spring greens or other green veg, sliced

2 eggs

Auntie Dang was a legend in the kitchen and showed me how to cook numerous dishes – her way, of course. She never followed a written recipe – it was all done by sight and would always vary slightly from the time before. One such dish was her version of stir-fried soy sauce noodles or pad see ew – perhaps not as well known as the ubiquitous pad Thai, but just as beloved in Thailand.

My version, based on her version, has been adapted over the years. Here I have used a carrot, not usually seen in pad see ew, and in fact, I often add an array of veg depending on what I have in the fridge. It might not be the done thing but I'm sure Auntie Dang wouldn't mind!

———————

Cook the rice noodles according to the packet instructions, then rinse well under cold water. Set aside.

Mix the soy sauce, oyster sauce and sugar together, and place near the stove.

Heat 2 tablespoons of oil in a large non-stick frying pan or wok over a high heat. Once very hot, add the beef. Stir-fry for 1 minute then add the garlic and fry for another 30 seconds or so. Add the carrot and green veg and stir-fry for another minute or two, until the greens have wilted.

Push the beef and veg to one side (if possible, move this side of the pan off the heat slightly), then crack in the eggs, adding a little more oil, if necessary. Leave for a few seconds, then scramble until the eggs are cooked. Add the noodles to the pan along with the sauce and stir-fry for a minute or two until well combined.

Remove from the heat and serve immediately. Feel free to add a drizzle more soy, to taste.

Spicy Pork Noodles

Preparation time: 20 minutes

Cooking time: 10 minutes

Serves 2

—

For the pork & marinade

2 cloves of garlic, crushed

2 tsp caster sugar

1 tsp grated ginger (approx. 2cm)

2 tbsp light soy sauce

2 tsp cornflour

½ a pork fillet (approx. 220–250g),
   very thinly sliced

For the stir-fry

1 tbsp chilli bean paste
   (see note, page 12)

1 tbsp light soy sauce

1½ tbsp caster sugar

100ml water

2 tbsp neutral oil, for frying

4 spring onions, cut into 5cm pieces

4 cloves of garlic, crushed

1 tbsp grated ginger (approx. 6cm)

1 carrot, cut into thin batons

2 portions of ready-to-wok
   udon noodles

To serve

spring onions, finely sliced

30g salted peanuts, roughly chopped

These spicy pork noodles are the business – full of fiery, umami deliciousness. I can't get enough of them.

The secret ingredient is chilli bean paste, which acts as a fabulous flavour bomb, adding a savoury depth and warm chilli heat. The end result is a seriously satisfying bowl of garlicky, spicy noodles that will leave you battling for the last spoonful.

Note: *Here I have used udon noodles, but other varieties would work equally well. Feel free to add whatever veg you have to hand.*

———

Mix the ingredients for the marinade in a shallow dish, then add the slices of pork. Combine well and leave to marinate for 15 minutes or so.

Meanwhile, mix together the chilli bean paste, soy sauce and sugar, then stir in the water. Have this sauce ready by the stove, as the stir-fry will cook quickly once you've started.

Heat 1 tablespoon of the oil in a large frying pan or wok over a high heat. Add the pork and stir-fry until browned (you'll finish cooking it later). Remove and set aside. Add another tablespoon of oil to the pan and stir-fry the spring onions for 30 seconds. Add the garlic, ginger and carrot and stir-fry for 1 minute. Add the noodles, then pour in the sauce. Stir-fry for a couple of minutes, making sure the noodles are properly coated, then put the pork back in. Cook for another minute, until the pork is cooked through, then serve immediately, sprinkled with the spring onion and peanuts.

Tangy Tamarind Noodle Broth

Preparation time: 5 minutes

Cooking time: 10 minutes

Serves 1

—

neutral oil, for frying

100g mushrooms, sliced

1 portion of ramen noodles

400ml veg stock

1–1½ tbsp tamarind paste
  (see note, page 15)

½–1 tsp dried red chilli flakes,
  to taste

1 tsp light soy sauce

1–2 tsp caster sugar, to taste

80g green veg, e.g. sugar snap peas
  or greens, thinly sliced

1 spring onion, finely sliced

Working from home means you have the luxury of making your own lunches, but it can be easy to get stuck in a rut or run out of time during a busy day.

This recipe for one is what you need when you're short of time but want full-on flavour. It's super versatile as well – swap out the mushrooms for cooked chicken or prawns, and use any veg you have in your fridge.

———————————

Heat ½ a tablespoon of oil in a medium-sized saucepan on a medium heat. Add the mushrooms and a pinch of salt, and fry for 3–4 minutes until cooked, stirring occasionally.

Meanwhile, cook the noodles according to the packet instructions, and place in a bowl.

Add the stock to the mushrooms, along with 1 tablespoon of tamarind, the chilli flakes, soy sauce and sugar. Bring to the boil, then lower the heat slightly. Taste and add the remaining tamarind and any extra seasoning, if needed.

Add the green veg and cook for another minute or two, until tender. Ladle the broth and veg over the noodles, sprinkle over the spring onion, and serve.

Peanut Hoisin Noodles

Preparation time: 15 minutes

Cooking time: 10 minutes

Serves 2

—

For the sauce

4 tbsp unsweetened crunchy
    peanut butter

3 tbsp hoisin sauce

3 tbsp chilli oil, with bits

1 tbsp lime juice
    (approx. ½–1 lime)

125ml water

For the noodles

1 tbsp neutral oil, for frying

1 pak choi or similar veg, sliced
    lengthways

1 carrot, cut into thin batons

½ a leek, sliced

2 cloves of garlic, crushed

2 portions of ready-to-wok
    udon noodles

To serve

30g salted peanuts, roughly
    chopped

1 spring onion, finely sliced

I'm a sucker for anything involving peanut butter, as you may well have guessed by now. Combined with hoisin and chilli oil it makes the most moreish sauce for noodles – and as an added bonus you can have it on the table in just 25 minutes.

Note: *This recipe requires chilli oil with bits, not just the oil.*

———————

Combine the peanut butter, hoisin sauce, chilli oil and lime juice in a small bowl. Slowly mix in the water, then set aside.

Heat 1 tablespoon of oil in a large frying pan or wok over a medium-high heat. Add the pak choi, carrot and leek and stir-fry for 1 minute. Add the garlic and stir-fry for a further 1–2 minutes.

Add the noodles and the sauce and combine well. Stir-fry for another 1–2 minutes, until the noodles are coated in the sauce and warmed through, then taste and season with salt, if needed. You may need to add a splash more water or a drizzle more chilli oil to loosen. Serve immediately, sprinkled with the peanuts and spring onion.

Miso Chicken Noodles

Preparation time: 15 minutes

Cooking time: 10 minutes

Serves 2

—

For the sauce

2 tbsp miso or white miso

1–2 tbsp honey (according to taste)

1 tbsp light soy sauce

1½ tbsp sriracha

50ml water

For the noodles

2 portions of medium egg or wheat
   noodles

1 tbsp neutral oil

2 spring onions, cut into 5cm pieces

2 cloves of garlic, crushed

1 tsp grated ginger (approx. 2cm)

1 chicken breast, thinly sliced

150g mushrooms, sliced

½ a head of broccoli, cut into small
   florets

To serve

1 spring onion, finely sliced

1 red chilli, finely sliced (optional)

A jar of miso is a storecupboard friend – just a spoonful adds a savoury back note to soups and broths, stews, stir-fries and even desserts. Here it creates a comforting and mellow noodle dish with a hint of heat from the sriracha. Simple and easy to make – just what you need midweek.

In a small bowl, combine the ingredients for the sauce and set aside.

Cook the noodles according to the packet instructions. Drain and rinse, then set aside.

Heat 1 tablespoon of oil in a large frying pan or wok over a medium heat. Fry the spring onions, garlic and ginger for about 1 minute.

Add the chicken and stir-fry for a minute or two until browned. Add the mushrooms and broccoli, and stir-fry for a further 2 minutes.

Add the noodles, then pour in the sauce. Cook for another minute or two, until everything is well combined and the chicken is cooked. Taste the sauce and adjust for seasoning – add extra honey, soy or sriracha, if necessary. Serve sprinkled with the spring onion and red chilli, if using, and eat immediately.

Thai Green Curry Noodle Broth

Preparation time: 5 minutes

Cooking time: 5 minutes

Serves 1

—

1 portion of fine rice noodles or medium egg or wheat noodles

400ml chicken or veg stock

1 tsp–1 tbsp Thai green curry paste (according to taste)

½–1 tsp sugar (according to taste)

½–1 tsp fish sauce (according to taste)

½ a carrot, cut into thin batons

50g cooked chicken or other leftover meat, torn or cut into small pieces

50g green veg, e.g. spring greens, chopped

To serve

coriander or spring onions, chopped (optional)

Another super-quick and easy noodle recipe to add to your lunch rota, and a great way to use up any leftover chicken or meat you might have. Thai green curry paste is a fantastic flavour hack used as the base for this warming and aromatic broth – completely different to the usual creamy Thai green curry but just as delicious.

Feel free to use whatever veg you have, and swap out the chicken for prawns or omit altogether.

Note: *Curry pastes vary hugely from brand to brand in terms of level of heat and salt, so add slowly and taste as you go.*

———————

Cook the noodles according to the packet instructions.

Meanwhile, heat the stock in a large saucepan. Bring to the boil, then lower the heat slightly. Stir in 1 teaspoon of green curry paste with ½ a teaspoon of sugar and ½ a teaspoon of fish sauce. Taste and add more curry paste, sugar or fish sauce as needed. If it's too spicy, add more stock.

Drain and rinse the noodles and place in a bowl.

Add the carrot, chicken and green veg to the broth and cook for 1–2 minutes, until the veg are tender and the chicken is hot through. Taste the broth and add any additional seasoning.

Ladle the broth, chicken and veg over the noodles, then sprinkle with coriander or spring onions, if using.

Spicy Beef Noodles

Preparation time: 10–15 minutes

Cooking time: 20 minutes

Serves 2

—

2 portions of medium egg or
  wheat noodles

neutral oil, for frying

1 onion, finely chopped

2 cloves of garlic, crushed

250g beef mince

100g spring greens, shredded

1–2 tbsp light soy sauce

2 tbsp rice vinegar

For the sauce

2 tsp chilli bean paste
  (see note, page 12)

1–2 tsp dried red chilli flakes

1 tbsp oyster sauce

2 tsp honey

To serve

1 spring onion, finely sliced

1 red chilli, finely sliced (optional)

These noodles are the happy result of another midweek fridge clear-out. Half a jar of chilli bean paste sat winking at me, along with a pack of mince bought with bolognese in mind, but not yet used. The combination, along with some honey and oyster sauce, transforms the beef into a caramelized, spicy number. Unctuous and mouth-wateringly good, especially when tossed with noodles (and some greens for balance).

———————

Cook the noodles according to the packet instructions. Drain and rinse under cold water, then set aside.

Mix the sauce ingredients together in a bowl, and set by the stove.

Heat 1 tablespoon of oil in a large frying pan or wok over a medium heat. Add the onion and garlic and cook for 5–7 minutes, stirring occasionally, until soft. Add another tablespoon of oil, then turn the heat up to high before adding the mince. Cook for a few minutes, until browned, breaking up the meat as you go.

Add the sauce and mix well. Cook for another 2–3 minutes, stirring occasionally, until starting to caramelize. Turn down the heat slightly and add the greens. Once wilted, add the noodles and combine well. Mix in 1 tablespoon of soy sauce and the rice vinegar, then taste and add extra soy, if needed.

Serve sprinkled with spring onion and red chilli, if using, and eat immediately.

Sides & Accompaniments

———

Peanut Serundeng

Preparation time: 5 minutes

Cooking time: 5 minutes

Makes a jar full

—

80g desiccated coconut

1½ tbsp caster sugar

50g raw peanuts, toasted
and roughly chopped

1 tsp ground coriander

½ tsp ground cumin

¼ tsp ground turmeric

½ tsp fine salt

2 tsp dried red chilli flakes

neutral oil, for frying

1 clove of garlic, crushed

Ten years ago I visited an Indonesian restaurant in a small town called Rijswijk in the Netherlands. I was with my Dutch granny, a long-time UK resident, who had been brought up in Indonesia as a child. We treated ourselves to a spectacular rijsttafel – literally meaning 'rice table' – made up of thirty small dishes. A feast! Of all the many taste sensations, the one that stuck in my mind was the serundeng. Sweet, savoury, spicy and crunchy. Perfect spooned on to rice dishes, curries and noodles – or straight into your mouth, as I have been known to do!

Place all of the ingredients (apart from the oil and garlic) into a bowl. Drizzle ½ a tablespoon of oil into a non-stick frying pan over a medium heat. When hot, fry the garlic for a few moments, then add the rest of the ingredients, stirring to ensure everything is well mixed.

Stir-fry for 3–4 minutes, or until the coconut is just beginning to toast, then remove from the pan and leave to cool.

Keeps for a week in an airtight container.

Gochujang Roasted Aubergines

Preparation time: 5 minutes

Cooking time: 45 minutes

Serves 2–4 as a side

—

1 medium aubergine

neutral oil

1½ tbsp gochujang paste

1½ tbsp honey

1 tbsp light soy sauce

2 cloves of garlic, crushed

1 spring onion, finely sliced

BC (before children!) I ate out regularly, always scanning the latest reviews to find new and exciting places, and doing my best to travel the globe while staying in London zones 1–3. I worked in central London, and looking back I was spoilt for choice.

It was nearly twenty years ago that I first set foot in a Korean BBQ restaurant, and what a joy to discover a whole world of food previously unknown. I particularly remember the pot of red sauce that accompanied the bibimbap. That sauce was, of course, gochujang.

Sticky, spicy, sweet and salty – this dish ticks all the boxes and then some. In this recipe I have combined it with honey, soy and garlic to create a punchy sauce with depth of flavour. It works brilliantly with the soft roasted aubergine, but it's also great with roasted cauliflower.

———————

Preheat the oven to 200°C/180°C fan/gas mark 6. Line a small baking tray with greaseproof paper.

Cut the aubergine in half lengthways, then, with a sharp knife, score the flesh deeply in a diamond pattern. Try not to pierce the skin. Place on the lined tray, drizzle each half with 1 tablespoon of oil, and sprinkle with sea salt flakes. Cook for 30 minutes.

Meanwhile, make the sauce. Simply combine the gochujang paste, honey, soy sauce and garlic. Set aside until needed.

Remove the aubergine from the oven and spoon the gochujang over each half, making sure to get the sauce into the cuts. Cook for a further 15 minutes, or until the flesh is cooked and meltingly tender.

Serve with the spring onions scattered over.

Chilli & Miso Stir-Fried Pak Choi

Preparation time: 10 minutes

Cooking time: 5 minutes

Serves 2

—

For the sauce

½ tbsp miso or white miso

1 tbsp oyster sauce

1 tsp caster sugar

2 tbsp water

For the greens

2 pak choi (or bok choi)

neutral oil, for frying

2 cloves of garlic, finely chopped

½–1 red chilli, finely chopped, to taste

A few years ago, I was offered a day's work experience at Som Saa Thai restaurant in Spitalfields, having previously met owner and head chef Mark Dobbie, and told him about my Thai heritage and love of cooking. What a memorable experience. I remember in particular watching one of the chefs cook stir-fried morning glory or pad pak boong fai daeng– with, fai daeng, literally meaning 'red fire'. The wok is heated at full throttle and the ingredients are thrown in, causing an explosion of flames. Not only spectacular but incredibly tasty too.

This is my take on that dish, substituting miso paste for the harder to find yellow soybean paste normally used. The flames might not be as high, but it's still delicious!

Note: *I've used pak choi here, but you could swap in spinach or other green leafy veg and just adjust the cooking time accordingly.*

————————

Mix the ingredients for the sauce in a small bowl, and place near the stove.

Prepare the pak choi. Cut the stalk into bite-size pieces and the leaves into wider strips. Heat a tablespoon of oil in a large frying pan or wok over a medium-high heat. Add the garlic and chilli and stir-fry for 30–60 seconds, until the garlic is just cooked. Be careful not to burn it. Add the pak choi and fry for a minute or two until just wilted. Add the sauce, coat well and turn off the heat. Serve immediately.

Garlicky Green Beans

Preparation time: 5 minutes

Cooking time: 3–5 minutes

Serves 4 as a side

—

neutral oil, for frying

300g fine green beans

4 cloves of garlic, finely chopped

Simple but effective. Charring the beans makes all the difference.

See photos on pages 94 and 127.

———————

Heat 1 tablespoon of oil in a frying pan or wok over a high heat. Once hot, add the beans and a good pinch of sea salt flakes, and cook until nicely charred, tossing occasionally. When they're nearly done, add the garlic and stir-fry for another minute or so, until the garlic starts to become golden. You may need to add an extra drizzle of oil to make sure the garlic doesn't burn. Remove from the heat and serve.

Spinach with Tahini Sauce

Preparation time: 5 minutes

Cooking time: 5 minutes

Serves 2

—

For the sauce

2 tbsp tahini

1 tbsp light soy sauce

1 tbsp rice vinegar

2 tsp caster sugar

For the spinach

2 tsp sesame oil, preferably toasted

250g spinach, washed and dried

Back when I worked in central London, I was a regular at conveyor belt sushi restaurant Kulu Kulu. I used to go there any opportunity I had, frequently on my own, to explore the delights of what was then a very new cuisine to me. Avocado and prawn tempura hand rolls and nasu dengaku – miso aubergine – were two of my favourites, along with spinach gomae – cold, cooked spinach in a sesame sauce.

This is my attempt at recreating the latter – the combination of the nutty, sweet-savoury sauce with the wilted spinach is a delight. I love it warm but it is just as delicious cold, as per the original.

See photo on page 153.

Note: *If serving cold, add the sauce at the last minute. Any leftover sauce will be delicious drizzled over green beans or broccoli.*

———————

Mix the ingredients for the sauce together in a small bowl. Set aside.

Heat the sesame oil in a large frying pan or wok over a medium heat. Add the spinach and fry for 2–3 minutes, or until wilted. Remove from the pan, leaving behind any excess liquid.

Place on a serving dish, drizzle with the sauce and serve.

Charred Corn
with Spring Onion Butter

Preparation time: 5 minutes

Cooking time: 15 minutes

Serves 4–8 as a side

—

neutral oil

4 corn on the cobs

50g unsalted butter

4 spring onions, finely sliced

1 red chilli, finely chopped

1½ tbsp caster sugar

1½ tsp fish sauce

Corn on the cob with a twist. The sweet-salty combination with the buttery spring onions is so simple, but deliciously unexpected. Perfect for barbecues, but easily done on the griddle at home, too.

———————————

Heat a griddle pan over a high heat.

Drizzle a little oil over each cob, then place in the pan. Cook for 10–15 minutes, turning occasionally, until nicely charred all over.

Once ready, make the spring onion butter. Heat a frying pan over a medium heat and add the butter. When melted, fry the spring onions and chilli for a minute or so, until starting to soften. Take off the heat, then stir in the sugar and fish sauce. Taste for seasoning, and add a pinch of sea salt flakes, if necessary.

Once the sugar has dissolved, drizzle the warm spring onion butter over the corn and serve immediately.

Roti

Preparation time: 20 minutes, plus resting time

Cooking time: 10-15 minutes

Serves 4

—

150g plain flour, plus extra
   for rolling

½ tsp salt

½ tsp caster sugar

2 tbsp neutral oil

90ml hot water

butter, for frying

Tip: *If you don't plan to use all the dough up at once, simply wrap it in clingfilm and store it in the fridge. It will keep for a couple of days. Just be sure to bring it back to room temperature and knead it for a couple of minutes before using.*

Yai Lott, my mother's grandmother, had a weakness for roti at breakfast time. Not just any roti, mind – roti fried in copious amounts of butter and served with lashings of condensed milk. Every morning at 5 a.m., my then ten-year-old mother was sent to the market to get first in line. She would watch in amazement as the Indian street hawker would toss the dough from hand to hand before frying it fresh before her eyes. Apparently, this was a common breakfast meal back then, but 'not very good for your teeth', my mother acknowledges now!

Rotis are, of course, also the perfect partner in crime to a saucy curry – just think of all that dipping and mopping potential. If you have a bit more time to spare while making dinner, I would highly recommend giving this simplified version a go.

See photos on pages 111 and 172–3.

———————

Combine the flour, salt and sugar in a large mixing bowl, then add the oil and 80ml of the water. Stir with a wooden spoon until a dough starts to form, then use your hands to gather it together. You may need to add the rest of the water if it's too dry. If it becomes too wet, add a little more flour. Knead on a floured surface for 3–5 minutes, until the dough springs back when you touch it.

If you have time, set the dough aside in a bowl and cover for 30 minutes. If not, proceed to the next step.

Divide the dough into 4 balls. On a floured surface, roll each piece into a disc, approximately 2mm thick. Place the discs on a plate, layered with greaseproof paper, ready to cook.

Heat a large frying pan over a medium heat and add a knob of butter. Once melted and hot, fry each roti until golden on each side, adding a touch more butter when you turn it over. This will take approximately 1–2 minutes on each side. Serve hot.

Turmeric Rice

Preparation time: 10 minutes

Cooking time: 35 minutes

Serves 4

—

neutral oil, for frying

1 large onion, finely chopped

2 cloves of garlic, crushed

1 tsp ground turmeric

1 tbsp medium curry powder

300g uncooked jasmine rice, rinsed

1 cinnamon stick

480ml veg stock

To garnish

2 tbsp neutral oil

2 onions, finely sliced

a handful of coriander leaves

Inspired by the rice element in the southern Thai dish khao mok gai – a biryani-style meal with chicken – this turmeric rice is comforting, earthy and moreish. Don't be surprised if you end up eating more than you bargained for – I usually do!

See photo on page 116.

Note: *To make the fried onion garnish even crispier, spread out on a baking sheet and place under a hot grill for a few seconds, being careful not to burn them. If using basmati rice, you need 225g of rice and 550ml of stock.*

Put 1 tablespoon of oil into a medium saucepan (that has a lid) over a medium heat. Fry the onion and garlic with a good pinch of sea salt flakes for 7–8 minutes, stirring occasionally, until softened.

Add the turmeric and curry powder and fry for a further 1 minute. Add the rice, stirring to coat all the grains in the spice mix. Add the cinnamon stick and stock, then stir and cover with a lid. Turn the heat up and bring to the boil, then turn the heat to low and simmer for 25 minutes, or until the liquid has been absorbed.

While it's cooking, make the fried onion garnish. Heat the oil in a large frying pan on a medium heat and, when hot, add the onions and a good pinch of sea salt flakes. Cook for 15–20 minutes, stirring occasionally, until the onions are golden and crispy. Remove with a slotted spoon and drain on kitchen paper.

Serve the rice with the fried onions on top and a scattering of coriander.

Stir-Fried Sesame & Chilli Kale

Preparation time: 5–10 minutes

Cooking time: 7–10 minutes

Serves 2

—

For the dressing

2 tbsp light soy sauce

1 tsp sesame oil, preferably toasted

1 tsp dried red chilli flakes

1 tbsp caster sugar

2 tsp rice vinegar

For the kale

neutral oil, for frying

100g kale, stalks removed, chopped

2 cloves of garlic, crushed

The nutritional powerhouse that is kale gets a makeover with these subtle but lip-smackingly good Korean-inspired flavours. Perfect served alongside dishes such as my Stir-fried rice with gochujang beef (page 135), Hong Kong-style rice pot (page 96), Stir-fried pork with basil (page 125) or Peanut hoisin noodles (page 151).

———————

Mix the ingredients for the dressing together in a small bowl, making sure the sugar dissolves. Set aside.

Heat ½ tablespoon of oil in a large frying pan or wok over a medium-high heat. Add the kale along with a splash of water and fry for around 3–5 minutes, stirring occasionally, until wilted and starting to char. Add the garlic and fry for a further minute or two.

Place in a serving bowl and add the dressing. Combine and serve.

Sichuan-Style Courgettes

Preparation time: 10 minutes

Cooking time: 15 minutes

Serves 2–4 as a side

—

1½ tbsp chilli bean paste
 (see note, page 12)

1 tsp light soy sauce

1 tbsp rice or white wine vinegar

1 tbsp caster sugar

150ml water

neutral oil, for frying

2 cloves of garlic, crushed

1 tsp grated ginger (approx. 2cm)

2 spring onions, finely sliced

2 medium courgettes (350g),
 cut into approx. 1.5cm slices
 on the diagonal

To serve

1 spring onion, finely sliced

Inspired by the Sichuan dish 'fish fragrant aubergines' – so named because of its use of flavours also seen in Sichuan fish dishes – this recipe uses courgettes instead, to great effect.

Smothered in a rich, spicy sauce, this is a fantastic way to showcase the unassuming courgette and make it the star of the show.

———————

To make the sauce, combine the chilli bean paste, soy sauce, rice vinegar, sugar and water in a bowl and set aside.

Heat 1 tablespoon of oil in a large frying pan or wok over a medium heat. Add the garlic, ginger and spring onions and stir-fry for 1 minute or so, until softened. Tip in the courgettes and fry for another minute or two, then pour in the sauce. Bring to a simmer and bubble for 5–8 minutes, or until the courgettes are just cooked, with some bite, and the sauce has thickened, stirring occasionally.

Serve sprinkled with the sliced spring onion.

Pickles & Condiments

Quick Cucumber Pickle

Preparation time: 5 minutes

Serves 4 as a side

—

4 tbsp rice or white wine vinegar

1 tbsp caster sugar, according to taste

½ a cucumber

I love a good pickle, and this one is super quick. Nothing like a bit of vinegary sharpness to add some vibrancy to the proceedings.

See photos on pages 32, 38, 90 and 187.

———————

Stir the vinegar and sugar together with a pinch of salt until the sugar has dissolved. You can either cut the cucumber into ribbons or slices. To make ribbons, using a peeler and a firm pressure, peel the cucumber lengthways. Or, cut the cucumber lengthways into halves or quarters, then slice.

Add the cucumber to the vinegar. You can eat it immediately or, better still, leave it to marinate for 20–30 minutes.

Cucumber Relish

Preparation time: 5 minutes plus 10 minutes cooling

Cooking time: 4 minutes

Serves 4 as a side

—

6 tbsp white wine vinegar

6 tbsp caster sugar

1 tbsp water

½ a cucumber, quartered lengthways and sliced

½ a small red onion, halved again and finely sliced

1 red chilli, finely sliced

1 tbsp coriander leaves, chopped

A variation on my Quick cucumber pickle, this more syrupy relish called ajad is often served with Thai fishcakes, satay and alongside various curries. One of the most memorable versions I've had was in a no-frills restaurant just off the Khao San Road in Bangkok over twenty years ago. It complemented my beef massaman perfectly, and was the first of many incredible eating experiences I had on that trip.

See photos on pages 24 and 186.

———————

In a small saucepan, heat the vinegar, sugar, water and a pinch of salt. Bring to the boil, stirring until the sugar has dissolved, then take off the heat and cool.

Put the rest of the ingredients into a small bowl and pour in the cooled syrup. Combine and serve.

Malaysian-Style Pickled Vegetables

Preparation time: 10 minutes

Cooking time: 10 minutes

Serves approximately 6

—

1 tbsp neutral oil

½ an onion, finely chopped

1 clove of garlic, crushed

1 tsp grated ginger (approx. 2cm)

½ tsp ground turmeric

¼ tsp dried red chilli flakes
(or just a pinch, if you
prefer it less spicy)

½ tsp salt

1 tbsp caster sugar

50ml rice or white wine vinegar

1 carrot

½ a cucumber

100g white cabbage
(equivalant of a small wedge)

Crouch End Hill used to be the home of a family-run Malaysian restaurant called Satay Malaysia. True to its name, the satay was bang on the money, but the dish that made the biggest impression on me was the Malaysian-style cold pickled vegetables, or achar. There are numerous variations of this dish in Malaysia, which vary from region to region. This is my attempt at recreating their version. Sweet, sour, spicy and surprisingly easy to make – if you're a pickle fan like me, these are a must have.

Delicious with my Dry beef and coconut curry (page 113).

See photos on pages 108 and 186.

————————————

Heat the oil in a frying pan over a medium heat. Add the onion, garlic and ginger and fry for around 5 minutes, until softened. Stir in the turmeric, chilli flakes, salt and sugar and cook for another minute, then add the vinegar and turn off the heat.

While this is cooling, prepare the vegetables. Cut the carrot into thin batons, cut the cucumber into eighths lengthways, then into rough 5cm pieces. Cut the cabbage in approximately 2cm slices, then roughly chop into 2–3cm pieces. Place in a large mixing bowl.

Pour the cooled onion mix over the veg and combine well. Cover and leave for a minimum of 20 minutes. If leaving for longer, place in the fridge to marinate. The pickles will keep for a couple of days, refrigerated, in an airtight container or sterilized jar.

Quick-Pickled Garlic & Ginger Carrots

Preparation time: 10 minutes + 15 minutes pickling time

Serves 2–3

—

3 carrots (approx. 200g)

1 clove of garlic, crushed

1 tsp grated ginger (approx. 2cm)

¼ tsp fine salt

½ tsp dried red chilli flakes

2 tsp caster sugar

A garlicky, ginger-infused pickle to pep up your meal. Delicious served with noodle stir-fries such as my Spicy pork noodles (page 147).

See photo on page 187.

Note: *Put into the fridge if leaving to marinate for longer than 15 minutes.*

———————

Using a vegetable peeler, peel each carrot lengthways to produce ribbons.

Place the ribbons in a mixing bowl and add the rest of the ingredients. Combine well, making sure the carrots are well coated. Cover and leave for at least 15 minutes before serving.

Clockwise from top left: Malaysian-style pickled vegetables (page 184), Quick cucumber pickle (page 183), Spicy pineapple pickle (page 189), Quick-pickled garlic & ginger carrots (page 185), Cucumber relish (page 183).

Quick Sweet Chilli Dipping Sauce

Preparation time: 5 minutes

Cooking time: 15 minutes

Makes approx. 130ml

—

150g caster sugar

75ml white wine or cider vinegar

2 tbsp water (30ml)

1–2 red chillies, finely chopped (depending on heat preference)

2 cloves of garlic, crushed

½ tsp fine salt

I often joke that I was weaned on sweet chilli, and although not entirely true, it certainly was an important addition to many of our meals. My mum would often serve up a rôtisserie chicken with a large bottle of sweet chilli for lunch – job done (it is actually known as nam jim gai in Thai, which translates as 'dipping sauce for chicken').

A bottle of the ready-made stuff is, without doubt, a great storecupboard cooking ingredient, but making your own is far less synthetic when we're talking about dipping and drizzling. Feel free to add a squeeze of lime if you like, and more garlic and chilli – this is just a simple base to get you started.

See photos on pages 33 and 34.

———————

Place all the ingredients in a small saucepan. Heat on medium-high and bring to the boil. Reduce the heat slightly and bubble for 10 minutes, stirring occasionally until reduced by about half. Taste and add any extra salt, if necessary. Pour into a sterilized jar while hot and put the lid on. Leave to cool completely, then store in the fridge, where it will keep for up to 4 weeks. If it becomes too thick, simply loosen with a drop of water or vinegar.

Spicy Pineapple Pickle

Preparation time: 10 minutes

Serves 2

—

1 x 4cm slice of fresh pineapple,
peeled and cut into small cubes
(approx. 1–2cm)

1 clove of garlic, crushed

¼ tsp dried red chilli flakes

2 tsp rice vinegar

a small handful of coriander leaves,
chopped (optional)

Sweet, tangy, zingy and spicy – this quick pickle-come-salsa adds a burst of vibrancy to any plate it adorns. The perfect sidekick to barbecues – think lamb chops, seared fish, barbecued chicken – as well as richer dishes such as my Dry beef & coconut curry (page 113). Or, for a simple dinner, why not try it served alongside pan-fried sea bass and my Garlicky green beans (page 168).

See photos on pages 79, 91, 112 and 187.

———————

Put all the ingredients except the coriander into a bowl and mix together. Add a pinch or two of salt, to taste. Store in the fridge until needed. Add the coriander just before serving, if using.

Two Fiery Thai Dipping Sauces

Thai Roasted Chilli Dipping Sauce

Preparation time: 5 minutes

Serves 3–4

—

2 tbsp lime juice (approx. 1½ limes)

2 tbsp fish sauce

1–1½ tbsp soft brown sugar
(according to taste)

1 tsp dried red chilli flakes

⅛ of a red onion, finely chopped

1 tbsp coriander, chopped

This is my take on nam jim jaew, a dipping sauce from north-eastern Thailand. Using dried chillies instead of fresh for a more roasted flavour, it is often served with marinated pork skewers called moo ping and would work with any barbecued meat, or with my Korean-style pork lettuce cups (page 39). The original version uses toasted and ground rice (which, although delicious, adds another step) and uses significantly more chilli – feel free to up the quantity if you're a chilli fiend!

Note: *If you don't have any red onion, simply use 1 spring onion instead.*

_____

Combine the first 4 ingredients in a small bowl. Make sure the sugar has dissolved, then add the red onion and coriander. Best eaten the same day.

Thai Chilli & Garlic Dipping Sauce

Preparation time: 10 minutes

Serves approx. 3–4

—

3 tbsp lime juice (approx. 2 limes)

2 tbsp fish sauce

½–1 tbsp soft brown sugar
(according to taste)

1 green chilli, finely chopped

1 clove of garlic, crushed

1 tbsp coriander, chopped

Known as nam jim seafood, this vibrant zesty sauce is served on tables across Thailand with all types of . . . you guessed it, seafood. I first had it doused over barbecued squid from a street food market in Bangkok, but it would be great with anything from prawns to seared tuna. Try it with my Prawn cakes (page 35) for added zing. Once again, the original features many more chillies, so increase the number if you so desire.

Note: *If you can't find green chillies, use red ones.*

_____

Combine all the ingredients and serve. Best eaten the same day.

Roasted Tomato & Chilli Dipping Sauce

Preparation time: 10 minutes

Cooking time: 5–10 minutes

Serves 2–4

—

3 medium tomatoes, halved

1 tbsp neutral oil

1½ tbsp lime juice (approx. 1 lime)

1 tsp fish sauce

¼ tsp dried red chilli flakes

⅛ of a red onion, finely chopped

a small handful of mint leaves, chopped

a small handful of coriander, chopped

½ tsp caster sugar (optional)

A barbecue is never a barbecue without at least one sauce (and most often three or four) on the table. I cheat with cooking in lots of ways, but will always find time to make a sauce for the barbecue table. Worlds apart from most shop-bought ones, they can really elevate a meal and can be easily conjured up. This dipping sauce, more like a salsa as we know it, would be perfect with a simple flat-iron steak, some chargrilled lamb, or fish such as sea bass or salmon. Barbecue season optional.

———————

Set the grill to high. Place the tomatoes in an oven dish and drizzle with the oil, a pinch of sea salt flakes and some black pepper. Grill for 5–10 minutes, until they are starting to char and soften.

Tip the tomatoes into a bowl with their juices and lightly mash. Add the lime juice, fish sauce, chilli flakes, onion and herbs. Taste and add sugar and extra seasoning as needed. Best eaten the same day.

Sweets

Miso Caramel Pears
with a Crumble Topping

Preparation time: 15 minutes

Cooking time: 20 minutes

Serves 2

—

For the crumble

60g plain flour

30g rolled oats

2 tbsp soft brown sugar

45g cold unsalted butter

For the pears & caramel

3 tbsp honey

1½ tsp miso or white miso paste

120ml milk

30g unsalted butter

2 ripe but firm pears, quartered or halved and cored

Salted caramel and I go way back. From fancy filled chocolates, to ice cream swirls, and best of all with just a teaspoon, I must have eaten litres of the stuff.

The addition of miso adds an umami saltiness that gives the caramel a rich depth of flavour and makes it all the more addictive (not that I needed an excuse!).

My cheat's version in this recipe works beautifully with pears, but would also be fantastic with slices of pan-fried apple.

Note: *Any leftover crumble topping will be delicious with ice cream or yoghurt. To serve 4, simply double the pear part of the recipe (the sauce may take slightly longer to reduce).*

———————————

Preheat the oven to 200°C/180°C fan/gas mark 6.

First, make the crumble. Place the flour, oats and sugar in a bowl, and rub in the butter until combined. Sprinkle the mixture evenly over a baking sheet and place in the oven for 15–20 minutes, until golden brown.

For the miso caramel, mix the honey in a bowl with the miso paste, then mix in the milk, making sure there are no lumps. Set aside.

Melt half the butter in a frying pan over a medium heat. Once melted, add the pears and cook for 5–10 minutes for quartered, 10–15 minutes for halved, turning occasionally, until the pears are golden, soft and cooked. Remove and set aside.

Add the remaining butter to the frying pan and, once melted, add the caramel mixture and gently simmer for a few minutes, stirring occasionally. The sauce should darken in colour to a light brown, and thicken to a syrupy consistency.

To serve, pour the miso caramel over the pears and top with a sprinkling of crumble. Delicious with a good dollop of ice cream.

Bananas
in Coconut Caramel Sauce

Preparation time: 5 minutes

Cooking time: 8 minutes

Serves 2

—

2 bananas, ripe but firm

a knob of butter

2 tbsp soft brown sugar

100ml coconut milk

a squeeze of lime juice

They caught my eye from a distance. Metre-long skewers loaded with tiny starchy bananas, barbecued until charred, then flattened in small bags and drenched in caramel sauce. A sweet, sticky mess of a dessert and a toothsome ending to the Bangkok street food feast we had just devoured. This is my home-style version.

———————

Peel the bananas and cut them in half across, then in half lengthways.

Place a knob of butter in a frying pan over a medium heat. Once it has melted and started to foam, add the bananas to the pan. Cook for a couple of minutes without turning, or until golden. Turn over and cook for another minute or so, until the other side is golden as well.

Carefully remove the bananas to two serving dishes. Add the sugar and coconut milk to the pan and bubble for a minute, or until the mixture thickens, turns golden and has the texture of single cream, swirling the pan occasionally, then add a tiny squeeze of lime.

Drizzle the bananas with the caramel. Delicious on its own or with a scoop of ice cream.

Miso Chocolate Fridge Cake

Preparation time: 15 minutes

Cooking time: 2–5 minutes

Makes 16 pieces

—

200g good-quality milk or dark
chocolate, or a combination of
both, broken into pieces

75g unsalted butter

3 tbsp golden syrup

1 tbsp miso or white miso paste

10 rich tea biscuits (or similar),
broken into small pieces
(about 85g)

100g raisins or other dried fruit
such as cherries or cranberries
(chopped if large)

80g nuts, chopped (e.g. hazelnuts,
pecans, almonds)

After being seduced by the addition of miso in my caramel, it was only time
before it found its way into one of my chocolate creations. A complete
chocaholic, I love it in all shapes and sizes, but this fridge cake has me
hooked. The miso is subtle but adds a rounded umami undertone to the
chocolate, which makes it ridiculously moreish. One piece is never enough!

—————————

Line a 20cm x 20cm tin with greaseproof paper.

Place the chocolate, butter, golden syrup and miso paste in a heatproof
bowl. Pour a few centimetres of hot water into a medium-sized saucepan
and bring to a gentle simmer. Place the bowl on top, making sure it doesn't
touch the water. Let the chocolate and butter melt, stirring occasionally,
until everything is combined.

Alternatively, place the bowl in the microwave and heat on medium for
1 minute. Gently stir, then heat for a further 30 seconds and stir again.
Repeat this process until the chocolate and butter have melted and
everything is combined.

Add the rest of the ingredients to the bowl and combine well. Pour into the
baking tin, press down and refrigerate for at least an hour, or until set. Cut
into squares and enjoy!

3-Ingredient
Coconut Ice Cream

**Preparation time: 10 minutes +
8 hours freezing time**

Serves 4

—

150ml double cream

200ml condensed milk

200ml full-fat coconut milk

coconut chips, toasted (optional)

Coconut ice cream will always remind me of sunny holidays in Thailand, and I often have a hankering for its creamy deliciousness, regardless of what the UK weather might be doing.

This cheat's recipe takes just 10 minutes to prepare and goes down a storm with guests – not to mention the kids (who have now sussed how to get into the freezer!). The perfect happy ending to an Asian-inspired feast.

———————

Place the double cream in a mixing bowl and whisk until it forms soft peaks. In a separate bowl whisk together the condensed and coconut milks for around 1 minute (if using an electric whisk) to aerate them.

Pour a very small amount of the condensed milk and coconut milk mixture into the double cream and gently stir in. Continue pouring and mixing in slowly until well combined.

Pour into a freezer container and freeze until set, around 6–8 hours depending on the depth of the container.

Remove from the fridge a few minutes before serving. Sprinkle over the coconut chips, if using.

Peanut & Coconut Bites

Preparation time: 10 minutes + setting time

Cooking time: 5 minutes

Makes 12–16

—

200g shortbread biscuits

120g butter, melted

120g desiccated coconut, toasted

160g unsweetened crunchy peanut butter

4 tbsp honey

50g good-quality white, milk or dark chocolate, broken into small pieces

Peanut butter lovers rejoice – this tasty teatime treat is for you! These easy no-bake melt-in-the-mouth bites are insanely good and have just six ingredients. A great recipe to make with the kids – not that you need that excuse!

———————

Line a 20cm x 20cm tin with greaseproof paper.

Place the shortbread biscuits in a large mixing bowl and bash them into crumbs, using the end of a rolling pin. They need to be fairly fine but they don't need to be perfect – some texture is OK.

Add the melted butter, toasted coconut, peanut butter and honey, and combine well. Pour into the lined tin and flatten.

Next, you need to melt the chocolate. Place the chocolate in a heatproof bowl. Pour a few centimetres of water into a medium-sized saucepan and bring to a gentle simmer. Place the bowl on top, making sure it doesn't touch the water, and let the chocolate melt, stirring occasionally. Alternatively, place the bowl in the microwave and heat on medium for 1 minute. Gently stir, then heat for a further 30 seconds and stir again. Repeat this process until the chocolate has melted.

Drizzle the melted chocolate on top of the shortbread mixture and refrigerate for an hour or so, until set. Cut into squares or rectangles and serve. Store any leftovers in an airtight container in the fridge – they will keep for up to a week.

Caramalized Pineapple Eton Mess

Preparation time: 10 minutes

Cooking time: 10 minutes

Serves 4

—

½ a fresh pineapple, peeled, cored and cut into wedges

3 tbsp caster sugar

300ml double cream

4 shop-bought meringue nests

3 passion fruit, halved

Eton mess is one of my indispensable summer standby desserts – so easy with shop-bought meringues – and importantly, always a plate-scraping success. Pineapple gives a tropical change to the usual berries, and when caramelized becomes something quite special. A stunning dessert, delicious at any time of the year.

——————

Put the pineapple and sugar into a medium-sized frying pan and heat on medium-high. Leave untouched for the first 2–3 minutes, then stir occasionally until caramelized and golden brown. This should take around 7–10 minutes, then set aside.

Place the double cream into a mixing bowl and whisk until it forms soft peaks. Be careful not to over-whisk.

Cut the caramelized pineapple into bite-sized pieces. To assemble, crumble the meringue nests on to a platter or four serving dishes. Dollop on the cream, then scatter over the pineapple. Spoon over the passion fruit seeds. Serve immediately.

Mango & Coconut Pots

Preparation time: 15 minutes

Serves 4

—

2 fresh mangoes, peeled and cut
   into pieces

2–3 tbsp honey

250ml coconut cream, chilled

coconut chips, toasted

A light and refreshing 4-ingredient dessert – perfect for summer days or after a big Asian-inspired meal.

———————

Blitz the mangoes with a stick blender or in a processor until you have a purée. Taste and add a teaspoon or two of honey, if needed.

Take the coconut cream out of the fridge and place in a large mixing bowl with 2 tablespoons of the honey. Using a hand whisk, whisk the coconut cream for 2–3 minutes, or until it looks like soft whipped double cream.

Place a spoonful of the mango purée in 4 small glasses or ramekins. Top each with a spoonful of the coconut cream, then repeat the layers until you've used everything up.

Top with the toasted coconut chips and serve immediately.

5-Spice Honey Apple Slice

Preparation time: 15 minutes

Cooking time: 12–15 minutes

Makes 8

—

4 tbsp honey

1 tsp Chinese 5-spice
(see note)

1 x 320g pack of ready-rolled
puff pastry

2 eating apples, thinly sliced

1 egg, beaten, or 2 tbsp milk

You've got to love shop-bought puff pastry for effortless baking. The Chinese 5-spice gives the honey-glazed apple an intriguing, yet subtle, aromatic back note. Perfect for elevenses, afternoon tea or as a light dessert.

Note: *If you've got a 5-spice powder with onion and garlic in the mixture (see note, page 13), use ½ a teaspoon of ground allspice instead.*

Preheat the oven to 220°C/200°C fan/gas mark 7. Line a baking sheet with greaseproof paper.

Place the honey and Chinese 5-spice in a small saucepan and cook on a low to medium heat for a couple of minutes, or until bubbling, stirring occasionally. Set aside.

Unroll the puff pastry and cut into 8 even-sized rectangles. Place on the baking sheet, spaced slightly apart.

Layer the apple slices on top of the pastry, then brush the apples with the honey, reserving a small amount for later. Brush the exposed pastry with the egg or milk wash. Place in the oven and cook for 12–15 minutes, until golden brown.

Brush the cooked apple with the remaining honey (you may need to gently warm it again if it becomes too firm).

Delicious served warm, with a scoop of vanilla or coconut ice cream.

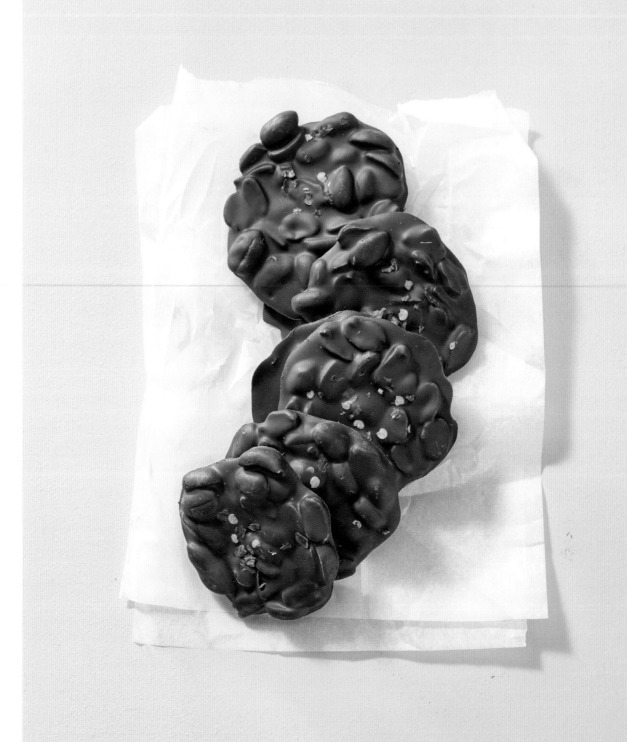

Chilli Chocolate Nut Clusters

**Preparation time: 10 minutes +
chilling**

Cooking time: 2–5 minutes

Makes 8

—

100g good-quality milk or dark
   chocolate, or a combination
   of both, broken into pieces

¼ tsp dried red chilli flakes,
   plus extra for sprinkling

75g salted peanuts

These 3-ingredient clusters combine my two loves – chilli and chocolate.
Salty peanuts are enveloped in a coating of chocolate and flecked with
chilli flakes for just the right amount of bite, making a devilishly addictive
after-dinner treat (or any time of the day for that matter).

Note: *You need to use chilli flakes for this, not chilli powder as I accidentally
did once. Unbeknown to me, the latter often contains other ingredients such
as garlic and cumin – an unwelcome surprise with the chocolate!*

———————————

Line a baking sheet with greaseproof paper.

Place the chocolate in a heatproof bowl. Pour a few centimetres of hot
water into a medium-sized saucepan and bring to a gentle simmer. Place
the bowl on top, making sure it doesn't touch the water, and let the
chocolate melt, stirring occasionally.

Alternatively, place the bowl in the microwave and heat on medium for
1 minute. Gently stir, then heat for a further 30 seconds and stir again.
Repeat this process until the chocolate has melted.

Once melted, tip in the chilli flakes and peanuts and combine well, making
sure all the nuts are coated.

Take dessertspoons of the mixture and spoon on to the baking sheet,
flattening them slightly into rounds, then sprinkle over a few extra chilli
flakes. Place in the fridge for approximately 20–30 minutes, or until
hardened. Best kept in the fridge.

Index

Author Bio

Half-Thai mum of three, entrepreneur and keen home cook, Dominique Woolf won the Channel 4 television show *The Great Cookbook Challenge with Jamie Oliver* in 2022. Having been a singer-songwriter and recruitment consultant in a previous life, Dominique decided to change careers and focus on her first love – food – after realizing just how much she enjoyed getting creative in the kitchen. She trained at Leiths School of Food and Wine to immerse herself in the industry and hone her skills, then became a food writer, before starting her own business, The Woolf's Kitchen, in the middle of lockdown 2020. Initially selling a range of sauces inspired by those her Thai auntie used to make, she has now expanded into chilli oils, pastes and nuts, too. Dominique is passionate about sharing her love of big, bold flavours and Asian-inspired cuisine.

Instagram: @dominiquewoolf

Twitter: @dominique_woolf

Website: thewoolfskitchen.com

Thank You

To have my scribbled recipes transformed into what you are holding now has taken the work of countless people. I am still pinching myself that I have had the good fortune to work with such a ridiculously talented group of professionals at the top of their game. This really has been a once-in-a-lifetime opportunity and I want to thank everyone involved from the bottom of my heart.

Without Jamie Oliver this would never have happened. Thank you doesn't quite say how grateful I am, but thank you, Jamie, for everything – for your mentorship, wise words, enthusiasm and support throughout – and of course for giving me access to your HQ and incredible team. Just wow. (Not to mention being the best sous chef I could have wished for!)

Thank you so much to my editor Rebecca Verity for taking me under your wing and guiding me through the whole process, and for being so organized and positive! And thanks to Jade Melling, too.

Thanks to my art director James Verity and photographer Richard Clatworthy for working your magic on the shoot and page, bringing my food and words to life. Rachel Young, Sophie Mackinnon and Ginny Rolfe – your food styling is pure artistry! Thank you for being so easy to work with and for making the shoot flow so well.

Thank you to everyone on the TV side at Jamie Oliver HQ. Thanks to Sam Beddoes and Sean Moxhay for your support and guidance. Just a big thank you to everyone for making me feel so at home.

Huge heartfelt thanks to the judges on *The Great Cookbook Challenge*, Louise Moore, Georgina Hayden and Jimi Famurewa, for believing in me and – Louise – for giving me this opportunity – I wouldn't be here without you!

Everyone at Penguin Random House – what an honour to be part of your stable. I can't thank you enough for such a warm welcome. Particular thanks to Ione Walder, Aggie Russell, Elizabeth Smith, Vicky Photiou, Ellie Morley, Amy Davies, Clare Parker, Ella Watkins, Deirdre O'Connell, Nick Lowndes, Lee Motley, Sarah Fraser, Dan Prescott-Bennett and Juliette Butler for everything you have done so far and for what lies ahead. Thanks also to Annie Lee, Eugenie Woodhouse, Jill Cole and Caroline Wilding.

I owe so much to Plum Pictures and Will Daws for creating and producing the show. To Phill Smith, Anita Goundar, Genevieve Welch and all the wonderful crew who were so lovely and made the filming experience a joy.

Of course, I couldn't have done this without the unwavering support of my friends and family.

Thank you to all my incredible recipe testers and cheerleaders – Jess Strong (who also played Ops Director to The Woolf's Kitchen while I worked on the book. You are a star!), Lotte Debell, Valeria Macchia and Robert Hart, Lisa Wilson Hardy, Katy Fattuhi, Marianne and Ian Mitchell, Ali and Joe Malone. Look what you helped create!

To my other amazing supporters who have believed in me from the start of my food journey – Laura Friederich, Nadia Hamila, Hilary Grierson, Anna Burdett, Toni Koppel, Marcelo Prado, Georgina Hartley.

Huge thanks to Amy La, Kristina Qureshi, Cherie Jones and Melissa Ng for your insights into your beautiful cuisines.

To my mum for instilling a love of Thai food and Asian supermarkets, and for teaching me how to taste as I cook. And importantly, so much love and thanks to you and Michael for going beyond your duty as grandparents and looking after the kids at the drop of a hat so I could work on this book.

Thank you to my dad for your unconditional belief in me and encouragement. Sorry I didn't include your cottage pie with baked beans – maybe in the next book! Thanks to my brother Sean for always being so proud of me. To my auntie Dang who inspired so much of this journey through her awesome cooking and *that* tamarind sauce. Thank you to my amazing in-laws Joyce and Lawrence Mitchell for your support and positivity.

Of course, none of this would have been possible without my husband Gordon. Thank you for your unconditional belief and support, for looking after the kids and being an all-round superdad, for giving me space and letting me loose in the kitchen, and for being the best sounding-board I could wish for. I'm so lucky to have you. And last but not least – biggest of hugs to my children Logan, Florence and Grace for (mostly!) giving the thumbs up to my cooking and for being the smiley, cheeky firecrackers you are.

PENGUIN MICHAEL JOSEPH

UK | USA | Canada | Ireland | Australia
India | New Zealand | South Africa

Penguin Michael Joseph is part of the Penguin Random House group of companies
whose addresses can be found at global.penguinrandomhouse.com

First published 2022

001

Colour reproduction by Altaimage Ltd
Printed in Latvia by Livonia Print

The authorized representative in the EEA is Penguin Random House Ireland,
Morrison Chambers, 32 Nassau Street, Dublin D02 YH68

A CIP catalogue record for this book is available from the British Library

ISBN: 978–1–405–95265–1

www.greenpenguin.co.uk